THE SINGLE MARKET IN INSURANCE

The Single Market in Insurance

Breaking down the barriers

ANDREW McGEE

Routledge
Taylor & Francis Group

LONDON AND NEW YORK

First published 1998 by Dartmouth and Ashgate Publishing

Reissued 2018 by Routledge
2 Park Square, Milton Park, Abingdon, Oxon, OX14 4RN
711 Third Avenue, New York, NY 10017, USA

Routledge is an imprint of the Taylor & Francis Group, an informa business

Publisher's Note
The publisher has gone to great lengths to ensure the quality of this reprint but points out that some imperfections in the original copies may be apparent.

Disclaimer
The publisher has made every effort to trace copyright holders and welcomes correspondence from those they have been unable to contact.

A Library of Congress record exists under LC control number: 98003168

ISBN 13: 978-1-138-36011-2 (hbk)
ISBN 13: 978-0-429-43329-0 (ebk)

Contents

vi *Contents*

Preface

Over the past ten years the Law of the European Union has moved at a rapid, sometimes alarming pace. The development of the 1992 Programme (which of course has continued well beyond 1992) has involved an enormous amount of legislation over a wide range of areas. Insurance law has certainly contributed its fair share to this mountain of paper. The result has been an extensive body of legislation and to a lesser extent case law which seeks to provide a framework for the development of a European Market in Insurance. As this book makes clear, much has been done, yet much remains to be done. However, much of what remains cannot be done by legislation: rather, it depends on the willingness and ability of businesses across Europe to make constructive use of the legislative framework. This is a salutary reminder for lawyers who believe that the answers to the problems of business regulation are to be found exclusively in legislation.

The book has taken a long time to write, partly because the landscape changed around me regularly as I struggled to describe it. I hope that some measure of stability has now been achieved, even if further legislative development seems inevitable. In general I have tried to describe the position as at 31 March 1997, though in a few places I have been able to add references to later events.

I cannot end without recording debts of gratitude where they are due. The European Institute of Public Administration and the European Law Academy both gave considerable practical help with this project. On the domestic front my wife Judith not only stoically endured my absences on research abroad and the many long hours I spent at the word-processor, but also read the proofs. My daughter Grace contributed to the whole process in her usual inimitable way.

ANDREW McGEE

1 Introduction

1. INTRODUCTION

Insurance is a very prevalent feature of developed modern societies. If Benjamin Franklin were alive today he would surely have to amend his famous dictum that the only certainties in life are death and taxation by adding insurance as the third.

It is scarcely an exaggeration to say that few people get far into adulthood without having an insurance policy of some kind. At the simplest level this may be a motor policy (compulsory for those who drive) or a household buildings or contents policy, the latter normally being obligatory for those who buy a property on mortgage.

In the field of life assurance, many mortgages are endowment mortgages, supported by a life policy, whilst investment insurance policies are very widely sold as savings vehicles, often in connection with private pension provision. The latter has greatly expanded since the changes in the law introduced by the Income and Corporation Taxes Act 1988 in an effort to begin shifting the financial burden of pension provision away from taxpayers generally and towards individuals. The most recent proposal by the UK government to phase out the existing state retirement pension and replace it with a so–called 'personal retirement account', to which individuals will be required to contribute during their working lives, will further accelerate this trend. In these circumstances the quality of insurance provision becomes a question of considerable general importance, and attention is necessarily focused on the legal regime regulating the provision of insurance services. Instead of being merely an arcane matter of technical provisions, this becomes a subject of vital interest to a great many people.

At the same time as insurance law and regulation has achieved this social importance, the nature and context of the subject has undergone very significant changes. At a domestic level the Financial Services Act 1986 introduced a new scheme for regulating the marketing and selling of investment policies, but even this Act, important and controversial as it was, is overshadowed in importance by the development of the Single European Market in Insurance, a development which forms the subject–matter of this book. To date the Single Market has concentrated on the regulatory aspects of insurance, and the schemes which it has created are explored in later Chapters. Some attention will also be given to the limited and so far unsuccessful attempts to address issues of insurance contract law.

Detailed accounts of the Single Market in Insurance are as yet in short supply. Ellis's book *The Single European Market and Insurance Law and Practice*[1] provides a good descriptive account of the position as it stood immediately before the implementation of the Third Directives, but because of its date was unable to provide any account of how those Directives were implemented into national laws. There appears to be no other thorough account of the subject, though Fitzsimmons has written about Insurance Competition Law.[2] The 1994 ERA Seminar on the Single Market in Insurance gave rise to a book of papers[3] which provides valuable insights into the subject. A limited,[4] though now steadily growing, periodical literature supplements these works.

2.   THE INSURANCE MARKET

In order to understand the workings of the Single Market in Insurance, it is necessary first to know a little about the way in which the insurance market has been organised and regulated. Insurance business is traditionally divided into a number of categories, though different categorisations may apply for different purposes. One very important division is that between long–term business and general business. Long–term business consists principally of life assurance, permanent health insurance and accident insurance, whilst everything else falls into the category of general business. The importance of this categorisation is that general insurance policies are normally for a period of not more than one year at a time, whereas long–term policies are normally capable of lasting and intended to last for longer periods. This has implications for the nature of the risk accepted by the insurer as well as for issues related to the formation of the insurance contract.

Another important division is that between indemnity policies and contingency policies. The former are those policies which are designed simply to make good losses suffered by the policyholder as a result of the insured peril. Contingency policies provide a specific sum on the happening of the insured event without reference to the loss suffered. To a large extent this division overlaps with that between general and long–term business, but permanent health policies are normally indemnity policies, as are some (but not all) accident policies. It should also be noted that in marine insurance, the

---

1   (1993) Wetherby, London.

2   *Insurance Competition Law* (1994), Graham Trotman, London.

3   *The Law and Practice of Insurance in the Single European Market* (ed.), McGee and Heusel, Bundesanzeiger, 1995.

4   Examples include Smulders and Glazier 29 CMLR 775, McNeill [1995] BJIBF 124, Butler (1996) 6 Int ILR 180 and Ruiz and Henin (1995) 5 Int ILR 156.

universal practice, sanctioned by statute[5] is for policies to be 'valued' policies, under which the value of the insured subject–matter is agreed in advance, that valuation being conclusive except in case of fraud.

Yet another way of dividing insurance is to distinguish between the compulsory and the non–compulsory policies. The former are found in those cases (of which driving a motor vehicle is the most important) where an activity may not lawfully be carried on without possession of liability insurance.

For other purposes marine insurance may be regarded as a separate category of insurance from all others because it alone has a codifying statute, the Marine Insurance Act 1906. However, it is clear that many of the principles set out in that Act apply equally to non–marine insurance, and the courts have been ready to refer to the Act for guidance even in cases not involving marine insurance.[6]

In the discussion which follows it will be seen that for regulatory purposes the distinction between life and other policies has been accorded by far the greatest significance.

3.   THE REGULATION OF INSURANCE[7]

Insurance as a service exhibits distinctive features which give rise to specific problems. It is in the nature of insurance that the insurer will take the premium in advance. Traditionally the whole premium was paid at the outset (other than in long–term policies where payment by instalment has always been very common) though in recent years instalment payment of premiums for general insurance has become more common. Certainly it is to be expected that the premium will have been paid in whole or in part before any claim arises. It is therefore essential to secure that those providing insurance services will be of sufficient competence at managing risks not to become insolvent between the payment of the premium and the date of the claim[8] and of sufficient probity not to misappropriate the funds which ought properly to be available to meet such claims. From a regulatory point of view these two

---

5   Marine Insurance Act 1906 s. 27.

6   The best recent example of this is provided by the decision of the House of Lords in *Pine Top v Pan Atlantic* [1994] 3 All ER 581, a non–marine case involving fundamental rules relating to non–disclosure, where their Lordships analysed the law almost entirely by reference to sections 18 and 20 of the Marine Insurance Act 1906.

7   Ellis (1991) 1 Ins L & P 74.

8   Or to have in place back–up schemes to compensate policyholders who suffer through such insolvency. In the UK this role is filled by the Policyholders Protection Act 1975.

concerns have been the major driving forces in legislation in the United Kingdom. That legislation began with the Assurance Companies Act 1870 and is now contained primarily in the Insurance Companies Act 1982 as amended, though some provisions of the Financial Services Act 1986 are also relevant.

The Insurance Companies Act 1982 imposes a regulatory system under which prior authorisation from the Department of Trade and Industry is required before carrying on insurance business. That authorisation will not be given unless the DTI is satisfied that the managers of the business are fit and proper persons for the purpose.[9] Insurance business is divided into a number of classes,[10] and separate authorisation is required for each class. It is possible and common to be authorised for only some classes of business.

The Act imposes requirements of financial solvency[11] on insurance companies in an effort to protect against the risk of insolvency. There are also ongoing accounting and supervisory arrangements, which may lead to the restricting or withdrawal of authorisation.[12] It is a criminal offence to carry on business without authorisation.[13] The system operated in the United Kingdom is widely regarded as being in practice a rigorous one. The Department of Trade and Industry does each year remove a small number of authorisations, either in relation to specific classes of business or in extreme cases for all classes of business. Behind the bare statistics of removed authorisations lies a great deal of work by the DTI in dealing with ongoing regulatory problems by means of information, advice, exhortation and threat. The success of the system may perhaps be judged by the relative rarity in modern times of financial collapse or grave dishonesty affecting insurance companies.[14] That perceived stringency, especially as compared with the attitudes *in practice* of the regulatory authorities in other Member States, exemplifies an important question about the development of the Single Market; if some Member States are thought by insurance companies to be more lenient in their regulatory practices than others, then there is, at least in theory, the danger that insurers will seek to operate in the most lightly regulated markets, thereby driving down regulatory standards.[15]

---

9   Insurance Companies Act 1982 s. 3–9; see Chapter 3 for the provisions of the First Directives in this area.

10 For details see Chapter 3.

11 Ss 32–35B.

12 Insurance Companies Act 1982 s. 11–13.

13 Insurance Companies Act 1982 s. 2.

14 The problems of the misselling of investment policies, discussed in Chapter 5, fall under the Financial Services Act 1986; they are not directly part of the regulatory environment for these purposes, nor are they the responsibility of the DTI.

15 Wills (1992) 2 Ins L & P 2; see Chapter 4.

It can be seen from the foregoing discussion that the system adopted, the essential features of which were in effect incorporated into European law when the First Directives were adopted,[16] is one of *ex ante* regulation, backed by ongoing monitoring requirements. Earlier legislation[17] had required insurers to deposit sums of money with the regulator as a guarantee against the consequences of insolvency, but this scheme has now been abandoned in favour of a more qualitative judgment of the fitness of those managing the business.

There is of course another very important aspect to insurance law, namely the law relating to the insurance contract itself. In the United Kingdom this is still for the most part a matter of common law, though Marine Insurance has been codified in the Marine Insurance Act 1906 and there are some other statutory provisions such as the Third Parties (Rights Against Insurers) Act 1930 which significantly modify the common law position. The common law of insurance is often perceived as being weighted against the insured,[18] a perception which has attracted the attention of the Law Commission, which in 1980 recommended reform of the most problematic part of insurance contract law, that relating to non–disclosure, misrepresentation and breach of warranty. In order to forestall this reform, the industry had to agree to the creation of the Insurance Ombudsman Bureau for the resolution of complaints involving personal lines policyholders.[19]

A second important point to be made is that English law, unlike the law of most other Member States, does not have requirements of *ex ante* approval of the terms and premiums applied to insurance policies. There is in this respect a clear contrast between the approach to questions of authorisation to carry on business and the approach to questions of insurance contract law. The validity of policy terms is not generally subject even to the scrutiny of the courts in England; the Unfair Contract Terms Act 1977 does not apply to contracts of insurance,[20] though the Unfair Terms in Consumer Contracts Regulations 1994[21] may allow some terms to be challenged in a limited range of cases.[22] For private policyholder the Insurance Ombudsman

---

16 See Chapter 3.
17 Assurance Companies Act 1870 and the Assurance Companies Act 1909.
18 Clarke, *The Law of Insurance Contracts* 2nd (ed.) 1995, LLP; McGee, *The Law and Practice of Life Assurance Contracts* (1995) Sweet & Maxwell, London.
19 The issues relating to this device are more fully discussed in Chapter 5.
20 *Ibid.* Sch. 1.
21 S.I. 1994 3159 implementing the Unfair Terms in Consumer Contracts Directive – Directive 93/13; note 58, below. See also Chapter 5.
22 See Chapter 5.

and PIA Ombudsman[23] systems may offer more prospect of challenging contract terms and/or the behaviour of insurance companies.

The approach of the EC to both the regulatory and the contractual aspects of the subject will be examined in later chapters.

4.   THE SINGLE MARKET CONCEPT

The history of the Single European Market project is well known and need not be recited here.[24] It is appropriate, however, to discuss some difficult issues relating to that concept. It will be recalled that the Commission White Paper on Completing the Internal Market[25] envisaged a situation where doing business between London and Madrid or Milan would be as easy as doing business between London and Manchester. In order to achieve this objective it would clearly be necessary to dismantle the three types of barrier traditionally recognised as impeding inter-state trade within the EC, namely the physical, the technical and the fiscal. Physical barriers raise few issues in relation to services, but fiscal and technical barriers are of obvious importance. As to fiscal barriers, it may be observed that there are significant differences in the taxation regimes applicable to insurance policies in different Member States. At the simplest level this may include taxes such as insurance premium tax in the United Kingdom. More complex issues arise in relation to long-term policies, especially investment policies, where the capital taxation of long-term gains in an investment fund differs between Member States.[26] Reform in this area raises vexed questions relating to the harmonisation of tax systems, which is perhaps the area where least progress has been made in the Single Market Programme. Technical barriers, in this case barriers to the entry of particular players into national markets, rather than issues about individual products, have of course been the most obvious stumbling block to the creation of the Single Market in Insurance. The history of the Directives designed to eliminate barriers of this kind will be found in Chapter 3. Indeed, the EC's legislative programme in relation to the Single Market in Insurance has given considerable attention to these two types. However, these are not the only barriers which impede the creation of a true Single Market. Aside from barriers of culture and language, which are without doubt very important, but about which the law can do little or

---

[23]   See Chapter 4.

[24]   Good articles on the general issues include Breder, R. 25 CMLRev 711; Schemers, H.G. 28 CMLRev 275; Everling, U. 29 CMLRev 1053; Forwood, N. and Clay, M. 11 ELR 383; Cremona, M. 15 ELR 283; Crosby, S. 16 ELR 451.

[25]   Com (85) 310.

[26]   Wills (1992) 2 Ins L + P 45.

nothing, there is also the major barrier created by differences in legal system between Member States. Even where a particular area has in theory been harmonised by means of Directives, there will usually still be differences in the detailed rules of different Member States. An additional factor, which is of especial importance in the United Kingdom, arises from the differences in conceptual approach between the common law systems and the civil law systems. These differences may cause businesses to be reluctant to enter markets where they will be unfamiliar with the legal rules and cultures operating and as such may in effect be a disguised barrier to inter–state trade.

The potential importance of this point cannot be overstated. If it is accepted that differences in legal system are an effective barrier to inter–state trade, then it must also be accepted that they are an effective barrier to the creation of a true Single Market. It would then follow that there can be no true Single Market until the laws of all Member States are not merely harmonised but made identical. There is of course no prospect that this will happen in the foreseeable future, since it would involve a massive centralisation of the law–making process within the EC; moreover, it would almost certainly mean the end of the common law system as it presently exists, since it seems overwhelmingly likely that in such a case the civil law system currently used in one form or another by 13 of the 15 Member States would prevail. This imbalance between common law systems and civil law systems will of course become even greater if the proposed expansion of the EU to include some of the former Soviet bloc countries happens as planned in the year 2000, since all these countries have now adopted codified systems based on the civil law. Unfortunately, the importance of the legal system barrier has not been widely recognised in discussions of the Single Market Programme, and it will be seen below that in the context of insurance no attempt has been made to address this problem (it is of course not at all clear what can be done to address it, especially on an *ad hoc* basis).

5.   HISTORY OF EC LEGISLATION

The EC has made relatively little attempt to address questions relating to insurance contract law. There was a Draft Insurance Contract Law Directive in 1979, but this was abandoned. The harmonisation of contract law across civil and common law systems is clearly a very difficult task and one which the EC has not attempted in areas other than insurance law. It was argued above that there can be no true Single Market in insurance (or possibly in anything else) without the full harmonisation of private law systems. This view has not in general commended itself to the EC. However, some modest progress in harmonisation of insurance contract law has been made, primarily in motor insurance, where Directive 84/5 has led to the harmonisation of the minimum liability cover required in motor policies[27] and Directive 90/232 requires motor policies to offer liability cover throughout the Member States, as well as harmonising rules relating to the Motor Insurers Bureau and its equivalents in other Member States.

On the regulatory side much more progress has been made. The main regulatory framework is found in the three generations of Directives, each containing one Life Assurance Directive and one non–Life Assurance Directive. This structure reflects the differing issues raised as between life and non–life assurance. There are also Directives on co–insurance[28] and on competition in the insurance sector.[29]

A. The First Directives

The First Non–life Directive[30] and the First Life Directive[31] began the process of harmonising the regulatory structure for insurance. They did this by introducing requirements for minimum levels of authorisation and supervision. All insurers must have prior authorisation[32] and must adopt an approved legal form (a limited company or its equivalent in other jurisdictions).[33] They must be effectively run by persons of good repute with appropriate professional qualifications or experience.[34] They must before commencing business submit a scheme of operations to the supervisory authorities,[35] must maintain adequate technical reserves[36] and an adequate solvency margin[37] and must produce annual accounts.[38] Insurers wishing to establish branches abroad must notify the authorities of their home state.[39] Indeed, the Directives adopt a fundamental principle, which is followed throughout the three generations of Directives, that all regulatory matters rest

---

[27] This was implemented in UK law by the Road Traffic Act 1988.
[28] Directive 78/473.
[29] Directive 92/3932.
[30] Directive 73/239.
[31] Directive 79/267.
[32] Art. 6 of each Directive.
[33] Art. 8 of each Directive.
[34] Art. 8(1)(e) of each Directive.
[35] Arts 8 and 9 of each Directive.
[36] Art. 24 of the non–Life Directive, art. 17 of the Life Directive.
[37] Arts 16 and 17 of the non–Life Directive, arts 18 and 19 of the Life Directive.
[38] Art. 19 of the non–Life Directive, art. 23 of the Life Directive.
[39] Art. 10 of each Directive.

with the insurer's home state, even where business is carried on elsewhere.[40] This choice of home state regulation is discussed further below.

B.   The Second Directives[41]

The Second Life Directive[42] and the Second non–Life Directive[43] develop the harmonisation process. They deal principally with the provision of services across national borders by insurers who do not wish to create a permanent establishment in another Member State. Life and non–Life policies raise somewhat different issues in this context and for this reason the two Directives diverge from each other rather more than was the case with the First Directives. In two important respects, however, they adopt the same principles. The first is that insurers wishing to provide cross–border services must first notify the authorities of their home state.[44] Whether they also need authorisation depended in the original form of the Directive on the nature of the business which they propose to conduct. In non–life business, where the risk was of a commercial character, no authorisation was needed, but where the risk was not of a commercial character authorisation by the authorities of the host state was required. This distinction was justified on the basis of the need to give greater protection to private policyholders. However, the implementation of the Single Passport system under the Third Directives, discussed below, has rendered this distinction obsolete. The second common feature concerns the question of the applicable law, where the starting point in both Directives is that the applicable law should normally be the law of the policyholder's place of habitual residence. In the case of the non–Life Directive this will be presumed to be the case if the state of residence and the state where the risk is situated are the same. If they are different, then either of the states concerned may be chosen. Both these principles are subject to the exception that an express choice of law, made with sufficient certainty and clarity, will be recognised if such a choice is accepted by the law which would under the above test be the applicable law.[45] Where the same policy covers more than one risk and these are situated in different Member States, the law of any of the states concerned may be chosen. In the Life Directive[46] the presumption is that the applicable law is the law of the state of the

---

40   Arts 13–15A of the non–Life Directive. Art. 15 of the Life Directive.
41   Bell (1991) 1 Ins L & P 85.
42   Directive 90/619.
43   Directive 88/357.
44   Art. 11 of the Life Directive, art. 14 of the non–Life Directive.
45   Art. 7 of the non–Life Directive.
46   Art. 4.

commitment, ie the state where the policyholder is resident, though the parties are permitted to choose the law of the state of which the policyholder is a national, should that be different. However, the Directive does not permit the choice of any other system of law. On the face of it these provisions show some concern for consumer protection by presuming that the applicable law will be the system with which the policyholder is likely to be most familiar. Unfortunately, this concern is somewhat undermined by the rules allowing the choice of other systems of law. Although such rules are quite normal in private international law, it seems likely that insurers offering policies across borders will want their own system of law to prevail and will draft the terms of the policy accordingly. Since such contracts are normally contracts of adhesion, policyholders will have no effective choice about the law which applies.

The Life Directive also has rules requiring a cooling–off period for cross–border policies,[47] whilst the non–Life Directive has special rules for compulsory insurance[48] and for co–insurance,[49] but these raise few questions of general interest.

When the Second Directives are considered together it can be seen that they mark an intermediate stage in the Single Market Programme. For the first time attention is given to the practical details of offering cross–border services, though the impossibility at that stage of devising a proper Single Passport system inevitably limits the degree of freedom conferred by these Directives.

C.   The Third Directives

The Second Directive provisions largely remain in force, but from a practical point of view they have been substantially overtaken by the Third Life Directive[50] and the Third non–Life Directive.[51] The two Directives in theory complete the Single Market in Insurance and they do so by creating a Single Passport system based on home country regulation. Insurers are required to be authorised by the regulatory authorities of the state in which they have their principal place of business, but that single authorisation gives them a passport to carry on business throughout the EC, subject only to notifying the authorities of any other Member State into which they wish to expand their activities. Those authorities have a residual discretion to exclude

---

47   Art. 15 of the Life Directive.
48   Art. 8.
49   Art. 26.
50   Directive 92/96.
51   Directive 92/49.

foreign insurers based on a concept of 'the general good'. This concept is not further defined in the legislation, and it may well be that any attempt to rely on it will result in a case before the ECJ, which will then have to offer clarification.[52] The deadline for implementation of these Directives was 1 July 1994, which was met in most, if not all, Member States.[53] It is believed that the necessary legislation is now in place throughout the EC.

D. Co–insurance

Directive 78/473 dealt with the position where legislation in a Member State forbade the insurance of a risk situated in that Member State by an insurer not established there. It required Member States to permit such insurers to join as co–insurers of the risk, though it was permissible to require the lead insurer to be established in the state where the risk was situated. The Directive has been rendered obsolete by the creation of the Single Passport system, since such prohibitions would now not be tolerated.

E. Competition

The question of competition within the insurance sector has also been the subject of some attention from the EC. Directive 92/3932 on the application of art. 85(3) of the Treaty to certain categories of agreements, decisions and concerted practices in the insurance sector deals with this matter. Subject to certain conditions art. 85(1) of the Treaty, is declared inapplicable in the insurance sector to agreements, arrangements and concerted practices which seek co–operation with respect to the establishment of common risk premium tariffs based on collectively ascertained statistics or on the number of claims; the establishment of standard policy conditions; the common coverage of certain types of risk; or the establishment of common rules on the testing and acceptance of security devices.[54] The more important of the conditions applying to this exemption are that standard tables and terms resulting from the collaboration must be for illustrative purposes only and their use must not be compulsory for any of the parties to the agreement; in the case of co–insurance and co–reinsurance groups there are limits on the combined market share in the relevant class of insurance which may be held by the participants

---

52   van Schoubreck, C., *The General Good* in McGee, A. (ed.), 'The Single Market in Insurance' ERA Trier 1995.

53   In the UK they were implemented by the Insurance Companies (Third Insurance Directives) Regulations 1994 S.I. 1994 No 1696.

54   Art. 1 of the Directive.

in the group – 10% in the case of co–insurance, 15% in the case of co–reinsurance.

The importance of this Directive in the context of the development of the Single Market in Insurance is by no means clear; it is not really intended as part of the Single Market Programme, being addressed more to competition issues than to Single Market issues. One possible Single Market effect is that it may facilitate the exchange of information between insurers in different Member States, though it is open to doubt whether at the present time such exchange is likely to be of major benefit to the insurers concerned, since policy terms (and probably claims experience and risk assessment) may well vary according to cultural and geographical factors.[55]

F.   Insurance Contract Law

There are no general Directives in force on the subject of insurance contract law, no further progress having been made with the draft insurance contract law Directive of 1979.[56] At the present time it seems unlikely that this area will be the subject of harmonising measures in the foreseeable future.

6.   HOME STATE REGULATION v HOST STATE REGULATION

As was mentioned above, the insurance sector has consistently adopted a scheme of home State regulation, ie regulation by the authorities of the State where an insurer has its principal place of business rather than host State regulation, ie a system of regulation by the authorities of each State in which an insurer carries on business, though the Third Directives also give host State authorities residual powers to restrict entry into their domestic markets. The choice between home State regulation and host State regulation is of considerable practical importance. Home State regulation offers the obvious advantages of relative administrative simplicity. Insurers need only a single authorisation (the so–called Single Passport) in order to be able to carry on business throughout the EC and are answerable to only one authority. On the other hand it is to be expected that differences of legal detail, as well as cultural differences, will lead to somewhat different approaches to regulation being adopted in different Member States. The consequence of this is that in any given Member State not all insurers will at

---

55   It might be thought, for example, that the experience of Dutch insurers with regard to flood claims would be of little interest to Swedish insurers, though this is no doubt an extreme example.

56   For the details of this proposal see Chapter 5.

any given time necessarily be subject to the same regulatory approach, since not all will necessarily share the same home State. This is likely to lead to claims of unfairness from those insurers subject to more stringent approaches and is also liable to cause confusion to customers, who cannot readily feel confident of the regulatory standard applied to any given insurer.

These two points raise the difficult question of the so–called 'Race to the Bottom'.[57] According to this theory the adoption of home State regulation is likely to lead businesses to seek to move their principal place of business to a Member State with a relatively lax regulatory environment, since that offers them competitive advantages over rivals who live under a more stringent regulatory environment. In the next stage of the 'Race to the Bottom' either all businesses in a particular sector will move to the laxest regulatory environment or individual Member States, wishing to attract businesses to their territory for legitimate economic reasons, will lower their regulatory standards in response to the competition. In either event the regulatory standards applied in practice will rapidly fall to the level of the lowest standards previously found (and, in theory, might fall even further if the competition intensifies). The potentially serious consequences for consumer protection if the theory is correct require serious attention to be given to the theory, which is in principle merely a rigorous application of the logic of competition. Despite its initial attractions, the theory is not without difficulties. First, it is not clear that all businesses in a given sector will want to take advantage of a laxer regulatory environment. There are no doubt short–term advantages in doing so, but it might be thought that well-managed businesses would be able to recognise the long–term advantages to be derived from a reputation for probity and integrity and would therefore scorn a suggestion of this kind. Indeed, it might even be thought that in an industry which needs to rely so heavily on concepts of good faith, the opposite phenomenon of a 'Race to the Top' might be encountered, in which businesses would want the presentational advantages of being seen to exist in a system with high standards. A second difficulty is that the theory assumes that businesses can fairly readily move the centre of their operations from one Member State to another. In the case of a small business with little in the way of central administration this might be true, but that profile does not at all fit the insurance sector, where businesses are large and where the role of central administration is substantial and depends on skilled staff. A German insurance company which proposed to move its principal place of business to Greece, might well find that few of its employees wanted to go with it (and if they did go, there might be serious language problems). Of course other moves might not raise quite such serious issues, depending on questions of distance, language and culture, but it is still clear that insurers do not always

---

57   Wills (1992) 2 Ins L & P 2.

have the freedom to move their principal place of business very readily. Aside from these theoretical questions, it is instructive to ask whether in other sectors of the economy there is any evidence of a 'Race to the Bottom'. It is submitted that there may be some modest evidence of this in relation to the United Kingdom. As is well known, the United Kingdom has been allowed a derogation from the Social Chapter of the Maastricht Treaty, and in some respects its level of employment protection is less than that prevailing in other Member States. The former Conservative government often claimed that this attracted inward direct investment. It is certainly true that some car manufacturers have moved some production to the UK in recent years, but it is unclear whether this is simply a question of lower costs or whether there are other reasons. Apart from that there appears to be no evidence that the 'Race to the Bottom' is happening on any significant scale. Of course this may be partly because the Single Market Programme has not yet developed to a stage where Single Passport schemes have been in place long enough to give rise to this effect. It may yet happen that the 'Race to the Bottom' becomes a serious issue.

In the light of this risk it might be thought that the idea of host country regulation merits serious consideration. It is obviously true that host country regulation would produce uniformity within each Member State. The overwhelming drawback of host country regulation is that it continues the historical partitioning of the Market along national lines, which runs completely contrary to the ideals of the Single Market. If host country regulation is to be rejected for this reason (as it is submitted that it should be) the question arises, how to manage a system of home country regulation so as to minimise the problems already identified. The answer must lie in ensuring a very tight co-ordination of the rules and practices in different Member States.

7.   THE PRESENT AND THE FUTURE

The harmonisation programme in insurance has been conducted by means of Directives rather than Regulations. This is a natural consequence of the fact that all Member States had insurance regulation in place before the programme began. Although the use of Directives does leave some freedom to Member States and does not create a monolithic system, it has been shown above that the three generations of Insurance Directives have in practice restricted quite narrowly the choices available to Member States. It might be thought that so tight a degree of regulation is incompatible with the principle of subsidiarity, but it is submitted that such a view is misplaced in the context of insurance. Subsidiarity requires only that decisions should be taken at the lowest level compatible with achieving the objectives of the

Treaty. However, it is surely clear that the achievement of anything approaching a true Single Market will require a high degree of co–ordination and uniformity in legal systems. It is therefore submitted that there is no good reason why Member States should be left in this context with any significant discretion beyond the choice of methods to achieve the necessary high standard of consumer protection. It might of course be thought that the same argument applies to virtually the whole of the Single Market Programme.

It has already been pointed out that the significant imbalances in insurance law arise on the contractual side rather than on the regulatory side. From that point of view it must be admitted that the harmonisation programme in insurance, so far has done nothing to redress that imbalance. However, the Unfair Contract Terms Directive,[58] which does apply to contracts of insurance, may go some way towards dealing with some of the more serious imbalances which exist within insurance contracts. On the other hand that Directive is not specifically aimed at insurance, and it is far from clear what effect some of its provisions will have in an insurance context.

The insurance Directives have not for the most part offered Member States the option of permanent derogations or a wide choice of regimes,[59] and this approach does not appear to have caused major difficulties. Although it is widely recognised that some Member States, including Germany, have found it difficult to open up their domestic markets to the prospect of competition, the Commission has been successful in negotiating texts which all Member States could accept without too much pain. This might give rise to the impression that there are no really serious problems in the creation of the Single Market in Insurance, or that Member States generally have displayed an uncharacteristic degree of selflessness. It is submitted that such a view would be unduly complacent. Insurance, even more than most other forms of business activity), is a sector where the substance is in the practice rather than in the legal rules. The standards contained in the Directives require Member States to have rules about the fitness of the managers of insurance businesses, for example, but it is inevitable that the fitness of individuals, always a matter of delicate judgment and not capable of being reduced to a formula, will be in the hands of civil servants in each Member State. In these circumstances it is to be expected that the standards applied in practice will differ according to the culture of the Member State concerned, so that there will not in fact be uniform regulatory practice. This simple example (and many others might be given) may help to explain why Member States are apparently relaxed about the

---

[58] Directive 93/13; Collins, H. [1994] 14 OJLS 229; Brandner, H.E. 28 CMLRev 647.

[59] In a few cases individual states have been allowed extensions of time for coming fully into line with the requirements of the Directives.

minimum standards of the Directives – they realise that the practical interpretation of these standards offers enough latitude to allow them to continue their pre–Directive practices, albeit under the guise of different legislative provisions. This would be of little importance if each Member State remained a separate market, but the prospect of a Single Market makes serious differences in regulatory practice a matter of some importance. It is as yet too soon to say whether the more cynical view will be proved to be correct.

Looking to the future, it is appropriate to ask whether the existing legislation is to be regarded as inward–looking or outward–looking; in other words, is it focused on the existing Member States or does it look forward to future enlargements. The answer to that may be seen as depending on the expected direction of future enlargement. At the moment a move into central and eastern Europe seems the most likely development. From this point of view the state of harmonisation in insurance (and probably in the whole area of financial services) does not bode well. It is based on the assumption of a well–developed and reasonably efficient sector of the economy, in which the importance of high standards of competence and probity is taken for granted. Clearly, these conditions do not prevail in the largely embryonic financial services sectors even of countries such as Poland and Hungary, which are likely to be among the first candidates from that geographical area for admission. The position may be somewhat more favourable in the case of other applicants such as Turkey and Cyprus. Unfortunately, it is very hard to see how this problem could sensibly be alleviated. There can be no question of lowering existing standards, and it would seem perverse to delay the harmonisation process on the ground that possible (but not certain) future members (at a date unknown) would face difficulties as a result of it. It would, however, clearly be necessary to allow central and eastern European countries a long period of acclimatisation and transition in this area.

The role of competition law in relation to the development of the Single Market in Insurance is also worthy of consideration. The one Directive to deal with this subject has already been discussed[60] and it can be clearly seen that breaches of the competition legislation have not preoccupied the Commission. It is submitted that the Commission is right to be relatively unconcerned on this point, since there is no evidence of collusion among insurers and no reason to suppose that the development of the Single Market will lead to such collusion.

Another imbalance which has been evident in the development of the Single Market in Insurance is that in most Member States consumer groups appear to have had little impact on the process, whereas the industry possesses a well–organised and powerful lobby for its own interests. The

---

[60]   Directive 92/3932, above.

limited scope of the regulatory scheme has already been mentioned, and, despite the important technical difficulties involved in adopting a more stringent scheme, it seems not unreasonable to suppose that industry pressure has had a certain amount to do with the decisions taken.

A major strand in the Commission's policy for the development of the Single Market has been the importance of encouraging and supporting Small and Medium–sized Enterprises (SMEs). However, nothing of this can really be detected in the harmonisation programme for insurance. On the one hand it might be said that encouragement of SMEs is not appropriate in an insurance context since virtually all the product providers are large companies or subsidiaries of very large groups; moreover, it is well known that the insurance market throughout Europe suffers from serious over capacity, so that the encouragement of new entrants to the market would achieve little of any practical value. Although this statement is true as far as it goes, it is submitted that it tells only half the story. Insurance intermediaries play a very important role in the making of insurance contracts, and many of these are SMEs (a significant number are sole traders, many of whom are in the industry for only a short time). The position of insurance intermediaries is often a difficult one, and it might be thought that here was a case where some positive action by the Commission could have been both valuable and popular. In practice, though, the Commission has been placed in a very difficult position, partly because the problems of the industry as a whole restrict what can be done for the intermediaries and partly because different Member States have radically different regulatory regimes for intermediaries. In these circumstances it is regrettable, but perhaps hardly surprising, that the Commission has backed away from any attempt to improve the lot of the intermediary. Indeed, the whole legislative programme is directed entirely at regulating the product providers, with nothing done for the intermediaries.

It may be noted that to date GATT has apparently had no impact on this sector. This is hardly surprising, given that GATT did not deal with services until the completion of the Uruguay Round. It remains to be seen whether the extension of GATT and the development of the World Trade Organisation will necessitate further liberalisation of the insurance market in Europe. It seems reasonable to suppose that other more controversial sectors will be the first to feel the effects of the new regime. It is also the case that the great majority of important providers of insurance in the world are within the European system anyway. The obvious exception is the North American market, and it must be from here, if from anywhere, that the challenge to the existing system will come. It is hard, though, to believe that insurance will be in the foreground of this challenge. The very existence of the WTO raises a serious question about the role and future of the Single European Market, which, in theory at least, must now be in danger of being subsumed into a

World Market; in the context of this global question insurance plays only a relatively small part.

The role of the courts, both domestic and European, in the development of the Single Market in Insurance has been somewhat limited. Before the Single Passport scheme got under way a series of cases known as the co-insurance cases[61] emphasised the freedom under art. 59 EEC to provide cross–border services on an *ad hoc* basis even in the absence of legislation implementing a full Single Market. In practice, though, these cases have been overtaken by subsequent Directives, and the ECJ and CFI have not been further troubled with questions relating to the Single Market in Insurance. Certainly, as discussed above, there is scope for some difficult questions to arise out of the Directives, but this has not happened so far. It may be supposed that it will happen only if individual Member States take a restrictive attitude to the Single Passport system and prove unduly ready to invoke the 'general good' exception.

Similarly, there is no evidence that national courts are being significantly burdened with regulatory questions of this kind. The exercise of the regulatory and supervisory functions is in effect a part of administrative law, and, in the UK at least, that administrative task is apparently not being exercised in an aggressive or confrontational way. At least two interpretations of this are possible. According to one interpretation it is evidence of good administrative practice and the good sense of insurers. According to a second, more cynical, interpretation it shows that the regulatory authorities are too lax in their approach to their duties. It is not possible to establish the degrees of truth attaching to either of these interpretations without a very detailed inside knowledge of the workings of the regulatory mechanism.

It is clear that the harmonisation of insurance regulation has had to proceed by means of positive harmonisation in view of the complexity of the subject–matter and the need for virtual uniformity between Member States. It has already been argued that positive harmonisation is in any event by far the most sensible way to develop the Single Market as a whole. The programme is in theory complete, and it is now possible to ask how rigorous the regulatory system is. An important point is that the regulatory system does not really deal with the nature and content of the products being sold, nor even to any significant extent with the methods by which they are sold.[62] It might be thought that this is evidence of a less stringent approach to

---

61   Case 220/83 *Commission v France*; Case 252/83 *Commission v Denmark*; Case 205/84 *Commission v Germany*; Case 206/84 *Commission v Ireland*, 4 December 1986; Lasok (1988) 51 MLR 706; Edward, D. 12 ELR 231.

62   Though of course the UKs own system, contained in the Financial Services Act 1986, does deal with marketing and selling.

regulation than would normally be expected in the case of goods. There is some truth in such a perception, since it is clear that legislation such as the Product Safety Directive[63] or the Toy Safety Directive,[64] which may be taken here as being typically of goods–oriented consumer protection legislation, are squarely aimed at the quality of the product. On the other side of the case it may be argued that techniques of regulation which are suitable for goods are not necessarily suited to services. In the specific context of insurance one difficulty lies in deciding how to determine the quality of a product. Different products may be suitable for different people and what is ideal for one may be quite inappropriate for another, whereas in the case of goods it is possible to specify minimum standards of safety (the Directives discussed above make no attempt to regulate the suitability of any product for any person). Moreover, it is in the nature of many insurance–based investment products that they are speculative, so that their true value cannot be known for some time after they are sold. In these circumstances it is almost impossible to have a quality test for insurance policies. This, however, is not a complete answer to the point. The UK has had to grapple with the same difficulties in its own regulation of marketing and selling of investment–based insurance products, and the solution adopted in the Financial Services Act 1986 is, to put a complex set of rules into very simple language, the adoption of a requirement that those selling the policies should satisfy themselves, so far as possible, at the time of sale that the product appears to be suitable for the needs of the particular investor. There is no requirement of European law that Member States must have rules of this kind, and this may be seen as a serious omission in the scheme of consumer protection.

So far this Chapter has considered the case of insurance in isolation from other sectors of the market. This was justified on the basis that insurance presents its own unique problems. Nevertheless, insurance no longer operates as a distinct sector of the market insulated from all others. In particular, it is necessary to consider those forms of insurance which are also investments in the context of the market for financial services as a whole. In this respect insurance may be compared with other forms of investment and savings. A person who is considering taking out an investment policy may also consider buying shares or unit trusts or may contemplate simply leaving the money in the bank or building society, perhaps using one or other of the forms of term deposit (some of them with special tax privileges) which these institutions can offer. The choice among these various forms of investment can often be a difficult one and it may not be obvious to the investor that he is dealing in a range of products which can have quite different regulatory regimes. From

---

[63]   Directive 85/374, enacted in the UK by Part I of the Consumer Protection Act 1987.
[64]   Directive 88/378.

the point of view of consumer protection as well as from that of internal coherence it is clearly desirable to have some degree of co–ordination among the various regulatory regimes. This point is reinforced when one considers that increasing numbers of companies now seek to offer many, if not all, of these services within a single group, a marketing and service concept known in France as *bancassurance* and in Germany as *Allfinanz*. In most cases regulatory constraints prevent a single company from offering more than one of these services, but the use of corporate groups, with one company for each of the services, effectively circumvents this problem. Although the segregation of the different services will no doubt be maintained at the formal regulatory level, it may be assumed that this segregation will not be emphasised in dealings with customers. In practice, development of the *bancassurance* concept in Europe has more or less coincided with the enactment and implementation of the various Directives in the financial services sector (though that is not to suggest any causal connection between the two) and a consequence of this has been that Directives continue to be addressed to individual sectors. The Banking Directives are not dealt with in detail here,[65] but it may be noted that they also have moved in the direction of a Single Passport system based on home state regulation. This does provide some measure of consistency, but a more detailed analysis of the respective provisions would be necessary in order to establish whether the underlying philosophies are the same and whether any significant differences in regulatory practice might be expected. One very basic observation, however, would be that the provision of banking services on a cross–border basis is far more advanced (partly because it is technologically relatively simple) than is the provision of cross–border insurance services. This also serves as a reminder that despite the obvious overlap between the different forms of financial service, they are also in other respects significantly different from each other, to the point where it should not be assumed that a single regulatory regime for all is either desirable or practicable.

8.   CONCLUSIONS

Although the legislative structure for the SEM in Insurance is apparently complete, it does not follow that the Single Market itself exists, not least for the reasons given above. It is clear that economic, social and cultural factors continue to be important. Certainly the United Kingdom has not yet seen a flood of foreign insurers seeking to take advantage of their new–found freedom. What has happened, however, is a different form of interpenetration

---

[65]   See Arora and Favre–Bulle, *The Single European Market and the Banking Sector,* in Howells, G. (ed.), 'European Business Law' (1996) Dartmouth.

of the market in that a number of UK insurers have formed strategic alliances by means of merger or the taking of substantial cross–shareholdings with insurers established in other Member States. This technique offers an easier way of obtaining a stake in the affairs of another insurer and an interest in the market of another Member State. At the same time it isan approach which has the potential to be anti–competitive, since insurers who have cross–holdings of this kind will naturally not want to enter directly the markets in which they have already achieved an indirect share.

Another important, but as yet unresolved question, concerns the willingness of policyholders to deal with insurers whom they may perceive as 'foreign'. In one of the more agreeable ironies of the Single Market Programme it appears that one of the situations most commonly giving rise to the purchase of insurance on a cross–border basis is that of civil servants seconded to work for the institutions of the EU in either Brussels or Luxembourg, who choose to effect their motor insurance with insurers in their home state and then use this insurance to authorise them to brave the roads of one of those two cities. The author is in possession of anecdotal evidence from some of these policyholders suggesting that the resulting dealings between insurers of different nationalities give rise to at least as many cultural misunderstandings as might be expected.

The Third Directives have now been implemented throughout the EC and the Single Market in Insurance has been in place for something over a year. But the process of achieving genuine interpenetration of markets will take much longer, assuming that it is to happen at all. The history of the harmonisation programme for the insurance sector teaches two principal lessons. The first is that even apparently complete harmonisation does not produce uniformity of law or practice throughout the Member States. The second is that the creation of a true Single Market is not something which can be achieved by legislation alone. It requires changes of attitude and culture within businesses. These changes may well not happen in our lifetime.

2 The Treaty Provisions

1. THE FOUR FREEDOMS

The European Union is built on the foundation of the so-called Four Freedoms, the right of free movement of Goods, Persons, Capital and Services. The Treaty of Rome, in its original form, contained very broad provisions recognising these freedoms, though it is fair to say that in the years between 1957 and 1985 the full extent of the freedoms conferred by the Treaty were not always recognised. The free movement of goods was the area in which most progress was made through the jurisprudence of the ECJ, perhaps because this is the area where the principles are easiest to state and where the Treaty contained provisions which were obviously capable of direct application.[1] Although some progress was made in relation to the other freedoms, it was only in 1985 with the development of the Commission's Programme for completing the Internal Market that real impetus was given to this process. Much of the Single Market Programme may legitimately be seen as the full working out of the implications of the Four Freedoms within the EU. In this sense it may be said that the 1992 Programme did no more than make explicit what had always been implicit within the original Treaty. The TEU, despite its immense political importance, does not make major changes in relation to the Four Freedoms.

2. FREE MOVEMENT OF SERVICES

Insurance is a service, and the provision of services within the European union is dealt with by arts 52–66 of the TEU. The major provisions of these articles are examined below, but it will immediately be clear that they do not by themselves provide an adequate framework for the regulation of insurance services.

However, the complexities of achieving free movement across all service sectors prevented the framers of the Treaty from conferring a simple across-the-board right to freedom in this area. Instead the Treaty sets out general principles, the detailed application of which is then left to further Directives

---

[1] General accounts of the law on free movement of goods may be found in most of the major European Law textbooks, such as Weatherill and Beaumont, *EC Law* (1993) Penguin, Kapteyn and van Themaat, *The Law of the European Communities* 3rd ed. (1994) Kluwers.

and Regulations. The Treaty provisions are considered in this chapter, whilst the detailed provisions of the Directives and Regulations will be considered in Chapter 3.

A. The Treaty Provisions

This section of the Treaty may be subdivided into those articles dealing with freedom to provide services and those articles dealing with the right of establishment.

B. Freedom to Provide Services

Arts 52–58 deal with the right of establishment. Arts 52–54 confer the relevant rights, whilst arts 55–58 deal with restrictions on those rights and other related matters. The basic provision is art. 52, which provides:

> Within the framework of the provisions set out below, restrictions on the freedom of establishment of nationals of a Member State in the territory of another Member State shall be abolished by progressive stages in the course of the transitional period. Such progressive abolition shall also apply to restrictions on the setting up of agencies, branches or subsidiaries by nationals of any Member State established in the territory of any Member State.

Freedom of establishment shall include the right to take up and pursue activities as self–employed persons and to set up and manage undertakings, in particular companies and firms within the meaning of the second paragraph of art. 58, under the conditions laid down for its own nationals by the law of the country where such establishment is effected, subject to the provisions of the Chapter relating to capital.

It is important to note that the Treaty gives no further guidance on what is meant by the term 'establishment'. This is a point of some significance, for the rules on establishment are different from those on freedom to provide services, discussed later, and the drawing of the line between the two categories is thus important. It will also be seen later that the ECJ has chosen to draw that line in a way which expands the category of establishment at the expense of the category of freedom to provide services.

Art. 54 requires the Council, on a proposal from the Commission, to draw up a general plan for implementing the objectives of art. 52. Thereafter, the Council is to proceed towards the overall objective by means of Directives.

Art. 54(3) gives further guidance on the principles to be adopted by the Council and Commission in carrying out these tasks. Some of these principles are relevant to the insurance sector. Principle (b) requires Council and Commission to ensure close co–operation between the competent authorities at national level in order to ascertain the particular situation within the Community of the activities concerned. This is inevitably important in any sector where there is already a substantial level of regulation at national level, which needs to be respected and harmonised in developing the Internal Market. Principle (c) calls for the abolition of those administrative practices and procedures the maintenance of which would form an obstacle to freedom of establishment. Again, this is relevant in areas which have established regulatory regimes, since it is quite likely that practices and procedures developed over the years will be found, on careful examination, to include aspects which are unnecessarily restrictive. Principle (f) calls for the progressive abolition of restrictions on freedom of establishment in all branches of activity; this is to extend to the conditions for setting up agencies, branches and subsidiaries in other Member States and to the rules relating to the entry of personnel belonging to the main establishment into managerial or supervisory posts in such agencies, branches or subsidiaries. The importance of the first part of this principle scarcely calls for comment, but it is also worth noting the second part of the principle. In a business such as insurance which relies heavily on the expertise of employees and in particular on their familiarity with the complex technical details of the product being sold, an enterprise which is unable to choose which personnel it will assign to branches and agencies outside its own home territory will thereby be placed at a significant competitive disadvantage. Finally, principle (g) calls for co–ordination to the necessary extent of the safeguards which, for the protection of members or others are required of companies or firms with a view to making such safeguards equivalent throughout the Community. Insurance, like other financial services, is an area where various safeguards are universally accepted as being necessary,[2] and this principle is therefore of obvious importance in the insurance sector.

The very broad nature of the freedoms described in arts 52–54 must be emphasised. The clear aim is to create an Internal Market without national boundaries, though at the same time these provisions, especially art. 54, recognise the considerable practical difficulties arising from this ambitious plan.

Art. 55 makes a very important exception to the art. 52 principles by declaring them inapplicable, so far as any Member State is concerned, to activities which in that State, are connected, even occasionally, with the

---

2   See Chapter 1.

exercise of official authority. However, this exception appears to have no relevance to the insurance sector, which in all Member States is apparently carried on entirely as a private sector activity. Even if a Member State were to operate an insurance company as a nationalised enterprise, it is not clear that this would amount to the 'exercise of official authority', a phrase which is not further defined in the Treaty.

The same article also authorises the Council, acting by qualified majority on a proposal from the Commission, to rule that arts 52–58 shall not apply to specified activities.[3]

Art. 56 allows a derogation from the general art. 52 principle in the case of national rules which provide for special treatment for foreign nationals on grounds of public policy, public security or public health. It seems unlikely that this article will be of major importance in the insurance sector. Although there will no doubt be specific cases where it is appropriate to object to the involvement of individuals in the conduct of an insurance business (a possibility expressly dealt with in the Third Directives).[4] Insurance is not a sector where blanket rules against foreign nationals could ever be justified.

Art. 57 deals with the question of mutual recognition of diplomas, certificates and other evidence of formal qualifications.[5] This is a potentially important area in the present context because in relation to some activities the laws of at least some Member States require evidence of proficiency before allowing individuals to undertake the activity in that Member State. It is necessary to ensure that qualifications obtained in one Member State are recognised in other Member States, since it could otherwise become effectively impossible for individuals to move freely between Member States to carry on the activity. Mutual recognition must of course take account of the need to ensure that all Member States set adequate and roughly comparable standards for particular qualifications. Within this constraint art. 57.1 calls on the Council to issue Directives for mutual recognition. The harmonisation of laws in this area is to be achieved using the co–decision procedure under art. 189b TEU.[6]

Art. 57.2 extends the idea of mutual recognition to domestic legal requirements governing the taking–up and pursuit of activities of self-employed persons. The co–decision procedure is to be used where the proposed legislation does not involve amendments to existing domestic law,

---

3   This does not appear to have been done in any case. Certainly it is clear that the provisions do apply in the insurance sector.

4   Art. 32.3 in both the Life and non–Life Directives.

5   For a general account of this subject see Schneider, H., *Anerkennung von Diplomen* Blackstone, 1995.

6   Art. 57.

but where such amendment is required, the Council must decide unanimously.

The question of mutual recognition does not appear to be of general practical importance for those directly employed by insurance companies, since such people are not generally subject to qualification requirements. The position may, however, be different in relation to insurance intermediaries, who may be subject to registration requirements[7] or even to authorisation requirements.[8]

Art. 58 equates the position of companies and firms (ie those constituted under civil and commercial law other than those which are not profit-seeking) with the position of natural persons by providing that companies and firms formed in accordance with the law of a Member State and having their registered office, central administration or principal place of business in a Member State are to be treated in the same way as nationals of a Member State. In the case of insurance the right of establishment and the right to provide services will in practice always be vested in companies rather than in individuals or un-incorporated firms, since the First Directives contain provisions[9] requiring insurance undertakings to adopt the form of a limited company.

The simplest form of the exercise of the freedom to provide services occurs where an insurance undertaking operates within a State other than its Home State without having any branch or permanent establishment in that State. On the one hand it might be said that this form of activity is of less concern to the authorities of the host State than is the case of establishment of a permanent presence. On the other hand it must be admitted that some serious issues can arise. Firstly, there is the question of which regulatory system is to apply to this activity – should it be a matter of host country control or of home country control. Whichever answer is chosen it is easy to see that the answer needs to be clear and to be consistently applied. Secondly, the occasional nature of the activity may give rise to as many problems as it solves, for the host country may not be very willing to deploy its full regulatory apparatus to deal with occasional provision of services, yet may equally not be happy to have insurers engaging in such occasional provision without being subject to the same rules as those with permanent establishments. The problem is exacerbated when it is remembered that operation in a Member State on a services basis does not by any means have to be an occasional activity – the only requirement in order to fall within this definition is that there is no permanent establishment within the Member State concerned. Thus, an insurer could in theory set up an office in an

---

[7]   Eg Insurance Brokers Registration Act 1977.
[8]   Eg Financial Services Act 1986.
[9]   Art. 8, as amended, in both the Life and non-Life Directives.

adjoining Member State, from where mail and telephone sales campaigns could be conducted into the Member State, without ever creating a permanent establishment in that State, and thus without ever falling within the right of establishment rules. This example immediately brings into question the soundness of making any absolute distinction between the services basis and the establishment basis, for it becomes clear that the damage which can be done to consumers by an incompetent and/or dishonest insurer does not principally depend on whether or not the insurer is established in the Member State where the services are provided.

C.   Right of Establishment

Arts 59–66 deal with the provision of services without establishment. The basic provision is art. 59, which provides:

> Within the framework of the provisions set out below, restrictions on freedom to provide services within the Community shall be progressively abolished during the transitional period in respect of nationals of Member States who are established in a State of the Community other than that of the person for whom the services are intended.

The Council may, acting by a qualified majority on a proposal from the Commission, extend the provisions of this Chapter to nationals of a third country who provide services and who are established within the Community.

Services are defined by art. 60 as extending to any services normally provided for remuneration (it is unclear whether 'normally' refers to the character of the services or the practice of the person providing them, though it is suggested that the former interpretation is more in keeping with the objectives of arts 59–66). Art. 60 goes on to create a further right, which is of considerable importance in the context of the insurance industry. This allows a person providing a service temporarily to pursue his activity in the State where the service is provided, under the same conditions as are imposed by that State on its own nationals. In effect, this provision allows an insurance sales person, for example, to provide investment advice and even to sell a policy in another country to a policyholder resident there, even though the sales person is not ordinarily authorised to carry on business in that other Member State. This right was not available to those who were in fact established in the territory of the Member State concerned, since such people were expected to rely on the right of establishment in so far as it applied to them. Before the enactment of the third generation of Directives, considered in detail in the next Chapter, this was a freedom of some importance, since it could allow insurers to circumvent host country controls on the conduct of insurance business, at least on an occasional basis.

Art. 61 paragraph 2 adds an important further provision of special relevance in the present context, by providing that the liberalisation of banking and insurance services connected with movements of capital is to be effected in step with the progressive liberalisation of movement of capital, which is dealt with in arts 67–73h.

Art. 63 is the equivalent of art. 54 in the previous Chapter of the Treaty, laying down similar principles to underpin a programme of measures aimed at achieving full freedom to provide services.

Art. 64 is a declaration of general intent in which the Member States affirm their willingness to extend liberalisation of services beyond the scope laid down in art. 63 if the general economic situation and the situation of the particular sector permit. The Commission is to make recommendation to Member States to this end. The article is expressed in such vague terms that it cannot possibly give rise to any specific enforceable obligations.

Art. 65 requires Member States to apply any surviving restrictions on freedom to provide services without distinction on grounds of nationality, whilst art. 66 makes the provisions of arts 55–58 applicable also to the right of establishment.

The question of the right of establishment gives rise to issues somewhat different from those presented by the simple freedom to provide services. A permanent establishment of an insurance undertaking in a State other than its Home State more naturally falls to be regulated by the host State than does a mere branch or agency or the provision of services on an occasional basis by a travelling representative, though, as was shown in the previous paragraph, this is a distinction which should not be insisted upon too strictly. In any event, the full programme for completing the Internal Market in Insurance has distinguished between freedom to provide services and right of establishment, dealing with the former in the Second Directives and the latter in the Third Directives. The Third Directives have adopted the principle of home country regulation rather than that of host country regulation, though some small residual powers are reserved to the host State. In practical terms it might be thought that the effective implementation of the right of establishment renders the freedom to provide services a question of largely academic importance. In fact, the Second Directive provisions remain largely in force, though it is true that the Commission is now considering whether to move towards a system in which both freedom to provide services and right of establishment are treated in more or less the same way.[10]

---

[10]   See further Chapter 7.

(i)   Free Movement of Insurance Services

It can readily be seen that the provisions of arts 52–66 provide only the most basic framework for the creation of freedom to provide services, much of the detail being left to be filled in by means of Directives applicable to particular sectors of the economy. In considering these Treaty provisions and the ways in which the Commission and the Council have discharged their duties under arts 54 and 63 it is necessary to understand the difficulties which affect attempts to secure the free provision of services across national boundaries but within the European Union.

Firstly, services raise different issues from goods. In the case of goods there will be a physical object moving across a national boundary, but in the case of services this will most often not be so. In the specific case of insurance the only physical cross–border movement is likely to involve proposal forms and/or policy documents (and in some cases even this may not happen). Since these are likely to be transmitted by post, or even in some cases by fax, there is no practical way in which their passage across borders can be prevented or even monitored. Thus, to put the matter in terms of the types of barrier to the exercise of the Four Freedoms which have commonly been identified, there is no physical barrier to the cross–border provision of insurance services. On the other hand, there may well be technical barriers, since the existence in all Member States of a system for regulating the freedom to carry on insurance business means that individual insurers may be unable to comply with technical requirements imposed by the authorities of a particular Member State. Alternatively, individual insurance products may be found not to comply with such technical requirements. The harmonisation of such technical requirements in order to reduce or eliminate this type of barrier, described in detail in Chapter 3, has necessarily formed a major part of the process of developing the Single Market in Insurance.

The third commonly recognised type of barrier, namely fiscal barriers, may also be relevant to services generally, since the provision of services may be subject to different tax regimes in different Member States. In the particular case of insurance further complexities arise because of the possibility of differential tax treatments for the policy document itself, for the premiums and for sums paid by the insurer in settlement of claims or on the maturity of an endowment policy. The recitals to both the second and the third generations of Directives recognise the existence of taxation differences as a possible distorting factor in the creation of the Internal Market, though there has as yet been no progress on the harmonisation of tax treatment. In practice it appears that differential tax treatment for the proceeds of investment policies has proved to be the major source of difficulty. Most systems recognise the need to avoid the double taxation of such proceeds which would arise if they were subject to tax as capital gains in the hands of the insurer and then subject to a second tax charge, either as income or as capital gains, in the hands of the policyholder. The logical solution to this problem is to exempt either the insurer or the policyholder from the tax charge, but logic alone cannot determine which should be exempt. It is perhaps not surprising that different legal systems have made different choices about this question. A policyholder living in a State which taxes the proceeds in the hands of the policyholder and who takes out a policy in a State which taxes the insurer instead, faces a double charge, whereas it appears that a policyholder who lives in a State which taxes the insurer and who takes out a policy in a country which taxes the policyholder, may escape liability entirely.[11] The resulting distortion of the market through capricious competitive advantages and disadvantages is obvious and clearly incompatible with the Single Market concept.

The fourth type of barrier, that represented by differences in legal systems, may also be relevant to any service, since the provision of a service will normally involve the existence of a contract, oral or written, and the private international law question of the law applicable to the contract is therefore likely to arise.[12] The problem is particularly acute in the case of insurance because of the extreme importance and complexity of the policy document. Prospective policyholders may find that their willingness to enter into contractual arrangements with particular insurers is affected by their lack of familiarity with another legal system. Similarly, given the considerable level of regulation which exists in relation to the process of selling and marketing policies, individual insurers may find that detailed differences between the systems of different Member States impede their activities by making it difficult if not impossible to have a single set of marketing literature which simultaneously meets the requirements of all the relevant authorities.[13] There has been no progress in attempts to harmonise the various national laws on insurance contracts, the 1979 Draft Directive[14] on that subject not having been taken up. The nearest approach to any attempt to deal with choice of law questions is found in the Second Directive provisions on determining the applicable law of an insurance contract; these do at least try to give policyholders some protection by making the law of the policyholder's habitual residence the applicable law in most cases.

---

[11] Wills (1992) 2 Ins L + P 45.
[12] For further elaboration of this issue see Chapter 5.
[13] In the UK such requirements are generally found in the Financial Services Act 1986.
[14] The Draft Directive on Insurance Contract Law OJ C190/2 28.7.79; see Chapter 5.

(ii)   Case Law

The most authoritative consideration of the practical application of these provisions in an insurance context came in *Commission v Germany*,[15] which concerned rules of German law purporting to limit the freedom of foreign insurers to sell insurance in Germany without having a permanent establishment there. A number of important points about the application of arts 59 and 60 EEC emerged from that case.

Firstly, a permanent presence in another Member State is in principle covered by the rules on right of establishment, rather than by those on freedom to provide services. This is so even where the presence does not take the form of a branch but consists merely of an office managed by the enterprise's own staff or by a person who is independent but is authorised to act on a permanent basis for the enterprise (ie what English law would describe as an agent). The line between cases subject to the rules on freedom to provide services and cases subject to the rules on right of establishment is a fine one, and this case emphasises how easy it is to fall on the establishment side of that line. The distinction is important because of the differences between the two sets of rules alluded to above. An enterprise which maintains an establishment (as here defined) in another Member State cannot in respect of that establishment take advantage of the rules relating to freedom to provide services.

Secondly, a Member State is entitled to restrict the freedom to provide services under art. 59 EEC in the case of an enterprise abroad whose activity is entirely or mainly directed towards its territory and which is thereby intending to evade the rules of conduct which would be applicable to it if it were established in the target State. This exemption is sufficient to deal with the possible problem of enterprises which establish themselves just across the border from the target State and then concentrate their activities on that State. To this extent it can provide some measure of protection against a possible 'Race to the Bottom',[16] but it is to be observed that it does not protect against an enterprise which establishes itself in the Member State which is perceived to have the laxest regulatory regime in the EU and then proceeds to sell insurance to a wide range of other Member States. In such a case no one Member State can claim that the enterprise's activities are directed 'entirely or mainly' towards its territory.

Thirdly, arts 59 and 60 became directly applicable at the end of the transitional period (1969 in the case of the original six Member States) and this direct applicability did not depend on the harmonisation or co-ordination of the laws of the Member States. These articles require the removal not only

---

[15]   Case 205/84 [1987] 2 CMLR 89.
[16]   See Chapter 4.

of all discrimination against a provider of services on the grounds of his nationality, but the removal of all restrictions on his freedom to provide services imposed by reason of the fact that he is established in a Member State other than that in which the service is to be provided. In particular, art. 60(3) aims to allow a service provider to offer that service in another Member State without suffering from discrimination in favour of nationals of that State. However, it does not automatically follow that all national legislation applicable to local nationals and the permanent activities of locally established enterprises may be applied to the temporary activities of enterprises which are established in another Member State. As an example of the difficulties in this area it is possible to contrast rules as to solvency margins on the one hand with rules as to technical reserves and conditions of insurance on the other. The First Directives contain enough rules on solvency to apply to the supply of services as well as to purely domestic provision of insurance. Consequently the authorities of the target State must accept as sufficient evidence of solvency a certificate of solvency issued by the authorities of the Member State of the main establishment. The same does not apply to rules on technical reserves and conditions of insurance, with the result that the target State is justified in imposing its own rules in these areas, provided that those rules do not exceed what is necessary in order to ensure the protection of policyholders and insured persons. The observations on this point are of course now obsolete in view of the Third Directive provisions on home country authorisation.[17]

Fourthly, national law requiring an insurer established in another Member State to have a permanent establishment within the jurisdiction and to obtain a fresh authorisation from the local authorities before he may provide insurance services there, is a restriction on the freedom to provide services, and is incompatible with arts 59 and 60 EEC unless there are imperative reasons relating to the public interest, and that public interest is not adequately protected by the rules of the State of establishment and the same result cannot be achieved by less restrictive means. These observations by the ECJ are of importance in the context of the discussion of the expression 'the general good', which appears in the Third Directives and is considered in Chapter 3. It is thought that the 'general good' is the same thing here as the 'public interest',[18] and the formulation of the public interest exception offered here by the ECJ is notably restrictive, taking into account the role of the State of establishment as well as the doctrine of proportionality. At the same time the ECJ goes on to acknowledge that in the

---

[17] As to which see Chapter 3.
[18] The original French expression is 'intérêt général'. The question of the General Good is more fully discussed in Chapter 4.

case of insurance services there are imperative reasons relating to the public interest which *may* justify restrictions on the freedom to provide services.

Fifthly, a system of prior authorisation for the right to provide insurance services, although an obvious restriction on the freedom to provide services, is compatible with arts 59 and 60, provided that authorisation is granted in accordance with criteria laid down by law and which are no more than is necessary for the protection of policyholders and insured persons. Moreover, restrictions imposed on insurers operating under the freedom to provide services may not duplicate equivalent statutory conditions which have already been satisfied in the State of main establishment. By contrast, a requirement that an enterprise must be established in a State before providing insurance services there is a complete negation of freedom to provide services and is therefore calculated to deprive art. 59 of all effectiveness. A requirement of this kind cannot therefore be accepted unless it is shown to be indispensable for attaining the objectives pursued. There is in fact no objective justification for such a requirement, since any legitimate objective in relation to the supervision of insurance business and the protection of policyholders and insured persons can be achieved by means of lesser restrictions.

This case was decided before the enactment of the Second and Third generations of Insurance Directives, and perhaps its most striking feature is the broad view which it takes of the rights and freedoms conferred by arts 59 and 60. Although, as has already been pointed out,[19] these articles are couched in general terms and appear to provide little more than a framework to be completed by means of Directives, the ECJ was prepared to hold that the articles became directly applicable on the expiry of the transitional period and were therefore capable of giving rise to rights and duties. It will be seen in the next Chapter that subsequent generations of Directives have developed the position in relation to freedom to provide services and right of establishment. The form which these Directives have taken may well be seen as having been influenced to a significant degree by the decision in this case and in particular by the views of the ECJ about the very limited nature of the restrictions on freedom to provide services which can be justified under the Treaty.

D.   Free Movement of Persons

Although attention has tended to focus on the free movement of services, it should not be forgotten that insurers may wish to pursue their rights under arts 52–66 (and particularly the right of establishment) by assigning workers

---

[19]   Pp 23–24.

to branches or permanent establishments in countries outside their country of establishment. Art. 48 TEU protects the right of workers to move from one country to another for the purpose of accepting offers of employment or to look for work. It does not in terms protect the position of a worker who is posted by his employer from one place of work to another. Freedoms of this kind are however, effectively guaranteed by Regulation 1612/68,[20] subject only to the limited exceptions provided for by art. 48, none of which is of general relevance in an insurance context.

E. Free Movement of Capital

This freedom may be of importance in an insurance law context, since the cross–border provision of insurance services is likely to result in the need for cross–border payments of premiums. It appears from the case law of the ECJ that the freedom to make payments for services is properly regarded as an incident of the freedom to provide services rather than as part of the free movement of capital.[21] The point is of importance because arts 52–59 are directly effective,[22] whereas art. 67 on free movement of capital is not.[23] The abolition of exchange controls throughout the Member States has apparently led to a situation in which this aspect of the problem is of no practical significance.

The question of payment is, however, only part of the free movement of capital, the other being freedom to make capital transfers for the purposes of investment. This does not seem to have been a major source of difficulty in the insurance sector. There have been cases of insurers buying substantial shareholdings in insurers established in other Member States,[24] but these have been cases involving companies listed on the relevant Stock Exchanges, so the general rules on freedom of payment have applied. In other cases it seems likely (though no empirical evidence is available) that exercise of the right of establishment and/or the freedom to provide services will not be capital intensive, since the major requirement is for an appropriately qualified workforce, which can be funded out of the income of the business. It is certainly true that existing discussions of the issues arising in the creation of the Single Market in insurance do not identify free movement of capital as a practical problem.

---

20   OJ L257 19.10.68.
21   *Luisi and Carbone v Ministero del Tresoro* [1984] ECR 377.
22   Co–insurance cases 205 and 206/84; see Chapter 3.
23   *Casati* [1981] ECR 2595.
24   See Chapter 7.

3 The Directives

The previous chapter showed the ways in which the Treaty provisions provide an essential framework for the development of the free provision of services but cannot by their nature deal adequately with the many different situations which arise in different service sectors. The detailed working out of principles for individual sectors has therefore been left to be carried out by means of Directives applicable to these sectors.

1. REGULATION

In the case of the insurance sector there have been three generations of Directives in the area of regulation, each generation containing two Directives, one dealing with Life Assurance, the other with non–Life Assurance. In each generation of Directives the same matters are covered by both Directives, the same principles being applied to their resolution so far as possible, allowing only for changes made necessary by the different characters of Life and non–Life business. The three generations of Directives are considered in detail below.

2. INSURANCE CONTRACT LAW

In addition to these three generations of Directives dealing with the regulation of the Insurance Market, there have also been some Directives dealing with the harmonisation of certain matters of insurance contract law.[1]

A. 1st Generation

The First generation of Directives[2] necessarily started from a very low base in terms of regulatory standards and common provisions, since prior to these Directives each Member State had simply adopted whatever solutions it thought fit to whatever problems it had identified in relation to the regulation

---

[1] For the details of these see Chapter 5.
[2] Directive 73/239 as amended by Directive 84/641 and Directive 90/618 (non–Life); Directive 79/267 (Life).

of insurance business. The following discussion refers primarily to the First non–Life Assurance Directive, though differences between the non–Life and Life Directives are noted where appropriate. The Life Directive covers[3] life assurance, annuities, personal injury policies when offered by life assurance companies and permanent health insurance policies (the last–named apparently existing only in Ireland and the United Kingdom). No undertaking may be authorised under both the First Life Directive and the First non–Life Directive,[4] except that undertakings already authorised for classes of business falling under both Directives at the time of the notification of the Directive are allowed to continue in that way provided that the Life and non–Life sides of the business are separately managed, subject to the power of the authorities of the home state of such an undertaking at any time to require it within a specified time to cease to carry on both Life and non–Life business within the same undertaking.[5] The apparent prohibition on the creation of new businesses carrying on both types of insurance is much less significant in practice than may at first appear, since it is possible to circumvent it by creating a holding company with two subsidiaries, one of which carries on Life business, while the other carries on non–Life business. This arrangement contravenes neither the letter nor the spirit of art. 13 of the First non–Life Directive, the purpose of which is to ensure that the management and funds of the Life business are not mixed with the management and funds of the non–Life business. The device of allocating the two sides of the business to separate companies achieves that objective.

All references are to the current text of the Directives, which have in a number of cases been modified by the later generations of Directives. In particular, the First generation Directives were extensively modified by the Third generation Directives. The concerns of the Commission at the time of the First generation Directives may be gleaned from examining the recitals to the First generation Directives. The more important points emerging from these recitals include: the need to eliminate divergences between national supervisory legislation, including in particular the need to make the provision of insurance services subject to a requirement of prior authorisation and the need to co–ordinate the provisions relating to the financial guarantees required of insurance undertakings, and in that connection the need to adopt a satisfactory system of classes of insurance. Two especially important matters are mentioned towards the end of the recitals. These are the need to provide that the rules on the taking–up or pursuit of direct insurance apply equally to all undertakings entering the Market, wherever their headquarters are situated and the need to include transitional provisions for the benefit of

---

3   First Life Directive art. 1.
4   First Life Directive art. 13.
5   First Life Directive art. 13.6.

small and medium–sized undertakings so as to allow them time to adjust to the new requirements.

Arts 6 and 7 of the Directive then impose the requirement of authorisation and define the classes into which insurance is divided for the purposes of authorisation. Arts 8–12 detail the administrative requirements for obtaining authorisation. The important aspects of these are that the business must take one of the approved forms (essentially a limited liability company),[6] must seek authorisation for one or more specified classes of insurance,[7] must submit to the regulatory authorities a scheme of operations[8] covering the nature of the risks to be covered, the guiding principles as to reinsurance, the items constituting the minimum guarantee fund, estimates of the costs of setting up the administrative services and the organisation for securing business. In relation to the first three years of the business the scheme must also show estimates of management expenses other than installation costs, estimates of premiums and claims, a forecast balance sheet and estimates of the financial resources intended to cover underwriting liabilities and the solvency margin. These provisions are intended to ensure that insurance undertakings setting up business make full disclosure of their intentions to the regulatory authorities and that they begin with a sound financial base and business plan.

Arts 13–20 of the Directive then deal with the conditions for exercise of business. The conditions stated in these articles are entirely concerned with financial supervision and accounting questions. They say nothing about questions relating to the ethical conduct of business,[9] nor do they deal with ensuring that the business is managed by fit and proper persons.[10] In their current form these provisions make all supervisory matters with which they deal the responsibility of the insurer's home State, in accordance with the general principle of home country control. Art. 13.2 provides that the concept of 'financial supervision' includes verification of the insurer's state of solvency, establishment of technical provisions and of the assets covering them. Art. 13.3 provides that the regulatory authorities in each Member State must require insurers to have sound administrative and accounting procedures and adequate control mechanisms. Art. 15 requires the imposition

---

[6]   Art. 8.

[7]   Art. 7.2.

[8]   Art. 9.

[9]   The Directives do not at any point require Member States to adopt conduct of business rules, though many Member States in fact do so.

[10]   Art. 37 of the First non–Life Directive makes limited reference to existing national rules of this kind, but does not insist that Member States should introduce such rules. In the UK the relevant provisions are in the Insurance Companies Act 1982 ss 60–64.

of rules to ensure that insurers have adequate technical provisions, which are in turn covered by matching assets. Under art. 20 the consequence of failure to comply with the technical provisions rules imposed under art. 15 is that the authorities of the insurer's home State may prohibit the free disposal of its assets, after communicating its intention to do so to the regulatory authorities of the States in which the risks are situated.

Art. 16 deals with solvency margins. Member States must require insurers whom they authorise to establish adequate solvency margins. The term 'solvency margin' is defined in art. 16.1 as being the assets of the business free of any foreseeable liabilities less any intangible items. The remainder of art. 16.1 lists in detail the matters to be included in the calculation of the solvency margin. Art. 16.2 explains in detail how the solvency margin is then calculated, offering two alternative bases, the premium basis and the claims basis. As the names indicate the former places more emphasis on the net levels of premium received in the last year, whereas the latter emphasises the amounts paid out by way of claims. Art. 16.3 sets out the calculations to be performed to determine the current solvency margin and imposes a minimum acceptable result. Art. 20.2 deals with the situation which arises if the calculation in art. 16.3 produces a result less than the minimum acceptable. In such cases the Member State must require that the insurer submit for its approval a plan for the restoration of a sound financial situation. If the authorities of the home State think that the financial situation of the insurer will deteriorate further, they may also restrict or prohibit the free disposal of the undertaking's assets. The measures taken must be notified to the authorities of other Member States in which the undertaking carries on business. These authorities shall, if so requested by the authorities of the home State, take the same measures in respect of assets within their jurisdiction.

Art. 17 then relates the guarantee fund to the solvency margin. The guarantee fund is one third of the total solvency margin, subject to specified minimum amounts for particular types of business. If the solvency margin falls below the amount of the guarantee fund (which would indicate a very serious financial situation for the insurer concerned) art. 20.3 requires the authorities of the insurer's home State to insist that the insurer submit a short–term finance scheme for approval. This requirement can be seen as part of a system of graded responses to financial difficulty experienced by insurers. An inadequate solvency margin calls for a plan to restore financial stability, but a solvency margin below the level of the guarantee fund calls for a more urgent and short–term response because it represents a greater degree of financial difficulty. The right to prevent free disposal of the insurer's assets is available in this case as it is in the less serious case where the solvency margin falls below acceptable levels.

Art. 19 deals with accounts. Member States are required to compel insurers whom they regulate to produce annual accounts covering all types of operation and dealing with its financial situation and solvency. Member States are required to give their supervisory authorities the powers and means necessary for effective supervision of insurers within their territory. Art. 19.3 goes on to list a number of specific powers which these authorities must have. These are: the power to make detailed enquiries about the insurer's situation and the whole of its business by gathering information or requiring the submission of documents concerning insurance business, carrying out on–the–spot investigations at an insurer's premises; the power to take any measures with regard to the undertaking which are appropriate and necessary to ensure that the activities of the undertaking conform with the laws of the Member State and in particular with the scheme of operations (submitted under art. 8) in so far as it remains mandatory and to prevent or remove any irregularities prejudicial to policyholders; the power to ensure that measures required by the supervisory authorities are carried out, if need be by enforcement, where appropriate, through judicial channels. In addition Member States may (but need not) make provision for the supervisory authorities to obtain information regarding contracts which are held by intermediaries.

Art. 22 lists the circumstances in which an authorisation to conduct business given to an insurer by the authorities of its home State may be withdrawn. These are: where the insurer does not make use of the authorisation within twelve months of its being granted or ceases to carry on business under the authorisation for more than six months (unless the law of the Member State provides for automatic lapse in such cases); where the insurer no longer fulfils the conditions for the granting of authorisation; where the insurer has been unable within the time allowed to correct a deficient solvency margin (or solvency margin below the level of the guarantee fund) in accordance within art. 20; where the insurer fails seriously in its obligations under the regulations to which it is subject. There is no further definition of the very imprecise concept of 'serious failure', the interpretation of which is therefore left to the authorities of individual Member States. It is to be observed that these are all cases which give the home State authorities a discretion to withdraw the authority. In none of these cases is the withdrawal compulsory. If the power to withdraw authorisation is exercised, the authorities of the home State must notify the authorities of the other Member States, who must take appropriate measures to prevent the insurer concerned from commencing operations in their territory under either the right of establishment or the freedom to provide services. The authorities of the home State shall take all measures necessary to safeguard the interests of policyholders and in particular are required to restrict the free disposal of the insurer's assets. Insurers are given some protection against arbitrary or unjustified use of the power to withdraw authority by art. 22.2, which requires the authorities exercising the power to give the insurer precise reasons for the withdrawal. Most developed legal systems then have some system equivalent to the English law concept of Judicial Review which would allow insurers aggrieved by the decision to challenge it before a court. It is to be noted that the First Life Directive contains a specific provision[11] requiring Member States to allow an application to the court in the case of a refusal of authorisation.

Arts 23–29 contain provisions dealing with agencies or branches established within the Community and belonging to undertakings whose head offices are outside the Community. Special rules are needed for such cases because the basic system of home country regulation is clearly inapplicable where the home State is not a Member State. Art. 23.1 lays down the basic principle that the setting up of a branch or agency by such an insurer must always be subject to official authorisation. Art. 23.2 lists the conditions which must be satisfied before the authorities of a Member State are at liberty to grant the necessary authorisation. These are that the insurers must be entitled to carry on insurance business under the law of its home State, must establish an agency or branch in a Member State, must undertake to establish at the place of management of the agency or branch accounts specific to the business which it undertakes there, must designate an authorised agent, to be approved by the authorities of the Member State where the agency or branch is established, must possess in that Member State assets of at least half the amount required for the guarantee fund under art. 17, must deposit one quarter of that amount as security, must submit a scheme of operations in accordance with arts 11.1 and 11.2 in the same way as an insurer with its head office in a Member State, must undertake to maintain a solvency margin, which must be of the same percentage as is required for any insurer under art. 16, though the assets and liabilities taken into account in calculating the solvency margin of the branch are only those relating to the business of the branch or agency concerned.

Arts 24 and 25 impose requirements of technical provisions and solvency margins similar to those applying under arts 16 and 17, but with the additional requirement that the assets and liabilities concerned must be situated in the Member State. Art. 26 goes on to create a derogation from the general principles of financial supervision for undertakings with head office outside the Community but which have established branches or agencies in more than one Member State. Such undertakings may apply to have its Community branches and agencies effectively treated as a unit, so that the solvency margin is calculated by references to all the branches and agencies

---

[11]   Art. 12.

combined instead of being calculated separately for each, the deposit of funds required under art. 23 is lodged in only one Member State instead of being required separately in each Member State where the undertaking has a presence and the assets representing the guarantee fund may be localised in any one of the Member States where the undertaking carries on business instead of being required separately in each such Member State. The application for the benefit of these privileges (which can only be granted jointly) must be made to the authorities of all Member States where the undertaking carries on business. One Member State must be named in the application as being in the future responsible for the overall supervision of the undertaking within the Community, ie taking on the role of *de facto* home State for the undertaking. The privileges may be granted only if the authorities of all Member States concerned agree, and must be withdrawn if a request to this effect is made at any time by the authorities of any Member State in which the undertaking carries on business.

Art. 27 applies the provisions of arts 19 (accounts) and 20 (failure to comply with requirements as to technical provisions, solvency margin or guarantee fund) to undertakings authorised under art. 23.

Art. 29A makes special provision for subsidiaries of parent undertakings governed by the laws of a third country and for acquisitions of holdings by such parent undertakings. The competent authorities in Member States are required to inform the Insurance Committee of the Commission of any authorisation granted to a direct or indirect subsidiary, one or more of whose parent undertakings are governed by the laws of a third country and whenever such a parent undertaking acquires a holding in a Community insurance undertaking which would turn the latter into its subsidiary. These requirements are in addition to all the pre–conditions for authorisation already mentioned.

Art. 29B deals with problems which can arise in the mirror–image situation of that above, ie where Community insurance undertakings seek to establish themselves in third countries. Member States are required to report to the Commission any difficulties encountered by their insurance undertakings in establishing themselves or carrying on their activities in a third country. The Commission is required to present to the Council at six–monthly intervals a report summarising the experiences of the various Member States in this regard. If the Commission concludes that a third country is not granting Community insurance undertakings effective Market access comparable with that granted by the Community to insurance undertakings from that third country, the Commission may submit to the Council proposals for the appropriate mandate to open negotiations with a view to redressing the situation. If the Commission concludes that Community insurance undertakings already established in a third country are not receiving national treatment offering the same competitive opportunities as are available to domestic insurance undertakings in that third country, the Commission may initiate negotiations with a view to remedying the situation. The differences between the two situations should be observed. When it is a question of obtaining authorisation, the only permissible response is to open negotiations to remedy the situation, and this requires the consent of the Council. When it is a question of discriminatory treatment against insurers already established in third countries, there is an alternative response of immediate retaliation, and this may be instigated by the Commission without reference to the Council. In such cases the Commission may also decide that the authorities of the Member States must limit or suspend their decisions regarding authorisation of direct or indirect subsidiaries of third country insurers and regarding the acquisition by such insurers of holdings in insurance undertakings with head offices in the Community. When taken on the initiative of the Commission these measures against third countries may not last for more than three months, though within that time the Council may decide to continue them.

If the commission considers that either of the above situations has arisen it may require Member States to notify it of any request for the authorisation of a direct or indirect subsidiary of a parent company governed by the laws of a third country and of any plans for such a company to become a parent company of a Community insurance undertaking.

Arts 30–32 contain transitional provisions on the coming into force of the Directive. Art. 30 requires Member States to allow undertakings already established in their territories at the coming into force of the Directive a period of five years to comply with the requirements of arts 16 (solvency margin) and 17 (guarantee fund). This period may be extended by a further two years in the case of the solvency margin for an undertaking which submits to the authorities a plan showing what steps it will take to bring its solvency margin up to the requisite standard within the additional two–year period.

Arts 33–37 are the Final Provisions of the Directive. Art. 33 calls on the Commission and the authorities of the Member States to collaborate closely for the purpose of facilitating the supervision of direct insurance within the Community and of examining any difficulties which may arise in the application of the Directive. Art. 34 requires the Commission to submit to the Council, within six years from the date of notification of the Directive, a report[12] on the effects of the financial requirements imposed by this Directive on the situation of the insurance markets in the Member States. Art. 35 imposes time limits (now expired) for the implementation of the Directive.

---

12   No such report has ever appeared in the Official Journal.

The first generation Directives must be seen in context. They had to start from a more or less blank sheet; before they were enacted there was no harmonisation of even the most basic matters in the regulation of insurance. They therefore have very limited aims, and must be considered in the context of the 1970s, when the term 'internal Market' was not in general use, and when it was clearly premature to think in terms of creating a genuine Single Passport system. On this basis it is readily understandable that they should follow the approach of other Directives of the time[13] by aiming for no more than the attainment of certain minimum standards by a process of harmonisation. In attempting this it was obviously desirable to deal with what were perceived as the most important and pressing aspects of the regulatory system. Thus, they deal with the process of authorisation, and in particular they co–ordinate the rules relating to financial stability. It was inevitable that authorisation should be the starting point, since everything else within the regulatory structure naturally follows from the basic authorisation process. It is also understandable, though perhaps not inevitable, that financial stability should feature high on the list of priorities. Such stability is one of the major objectives of any system of financial services regulation, and failure to address this point would have exposed the first Directive regime to serious criticism in the event of failure of major insurers. At the same time it is clear that the First Directives cannot be regarded as being aimed at creating the Internal Market, since they do not attempt to deal with issues about the cross–border provision of services or the right of establishment. Despite their limited aims they represent the essential first step in applying the principles of arts 52–66 to the insurance sector. They provide the foundation on which subsequent generations of Directives have been able to build.

B. 2nd Generation

The Second generation of Directives[14] dealt with a number of matters relating to the provision of services on a cross–border basis but not to the right of establishment, Again, this account is based on the non–Life Directive, but relevant differences in the Life Directive are noted.

First, it is helpful to draw attention to a few of the statements made in the recitals to this Directive, which give some indication of the thinking

---

[13] The company law Directives provide a good example.
[14] Directive 88/357 as amended by Directive 90/618 (non–Life); Directive 90/619 (Life).

behind the substantive provisions and of the context in which the Directive was prepared.

One significant recital is that which declares the desirability of separating the treatment of the right of establishment from the right of free provision of services. It is of course true that the Treaty provisions[15] make this distinction, but the recital gives no reasoned argument to show why in this particular context it is appropriate to treat them differently. The importance of this point may be seen in Chapter 7, where it will be apparent that the Commission, in its recent Green Book, is increasingly struggling with the practical and theoretical issues relating to this distinction.

A later recital refers to difficulties caused by differences in the tax regimes applicable to insurance contracts in different Member States, some imposing no charge on policies but most imposing some form of indirect taxation. The recital refers to the obvious danger that these differences may lead to distortion in the pattern of competition within the Member States and suggests that the adoption of the system of taxation prevailing in the Member State where the risk is situated is best adapted to remedying this problem pending any future harmonisation of tax regimes.

The early articles of the Directive provide definitions of a number of very important concepts for the development of the Internal Market in Insurance. Art. 2 defines the 'Member State where the risk is situated' an expression used later in the Directive in determining questions about the proper law of the policy. The definition distinguishes between different types of policy and is worth detailed attention. The general rule is that the risk is considered to be situated in the Member State where the policyholder has his habitual residence, or, if the policyholder is a legal person, where his establishment to which the policy relates is situated. The effect of this rule will normally be to ensure that the policy is subject to the system of law with which the policyholder is likely to be most familiar. However, the exceptions to this general principle are also important. In the case of a buildings policy or a combined buildings and contents policy the risk is situated in the country where the property is situated. This reflects the general rule of private international law that in cases of immovable property the proper law is normally the *lex situs*, but it also has the effect that in these cases the applicable law may not be the law with which the policyholder is most familiar.

Where the insurance relates to any type of vehicle, the risk is situated in the Member State where the vehicle is registered. This creates the possibility that the risk could be situated in different Member States for two or more

---

15   Arts 52–59; see Chapter 2.

vehicles insured under the same policy but registered in different Member States.

In the case of travel or holiday risks where the policy lasts for four months or less the risk is situated in the country where the policy was taken out, even if, as will commonly be the case, the holiday is to be taken in another country.

These provisions have to be understood in conjunction with art. 7 of the Directive, which lays down the principles for determining the law applicable to contracts of insurance. The simplest case occurs where the policyholder has his habitual residence[16] in the State where the risk is situated. In this case the law of that Member State is presumed to be the applicable law. However, the parties may choose to apply the law of another Member State where the law of the State in which the risk is situated allows them to do so. In the typical case, certainly in most cases where the policyholder is an individual, the choice of another system of law is unlikely to be appropriate. However, English law does generally recognise the freedom of contracting parties to choose which law shall apply to their contract, and it would be possible for an insurer established in another country to produce a policy document which contained an express choice of law clause nominating the law of the insurer's home State. Obviously, the choice of an alternative applicable law requires the consent of both parties, but the application form for the policy will normally be drafted (by the insurer) as a request for insurance on the insurer's standard terms. This situation is to some extent dealt with by paragraph (g) of art. 7.1, which states that an express choice of law shall not override mandatory rules of Member States forbidding the choice of another legal system when all the other elements of the contract point to a connection with only one Member State. However, English law has no such rule, the relevant rule of English law being only that the express choice of law must be made *bona fide*.[17]

Where the policyholder's habitual residence is not in the State where the risk is situated, the parties may choose to apply either the law of the policyholder's habitual residence or the law of the State where the risk is situated. This paragraph of the article does not say what will happen if the policy makes no express choice as between these options. In terms of the general principles of private international law, which are declared by art. 7.3 to be applicable in the absence of any express provision in the Directive, the answer ought to be that the applicable law is that of the country with which

---

16 Throughout the following discussion the term 'habitual residence', which is strictly applicable only to individuals, is used to refer also to the central administration of a legal person.

17 *Vita Food Products Inc v Unus Shipping Co* [1939] A.C. 277 P.C.

the contract has its closest connection. This principle is introduced into the Directive by paragraph (h) of art. 7.1. However, this leaves open the question, with which country is the contract considered to have its closest connection? So far as English private international law is concerned, the place where the contract is entered into is commonly taken as a significant consideration in answering this question.[18] Similarly an express choice of jurisdiction will often be regarded as pointing towards an implied choice of law, even though jurisdiction and choice of law are logically distinct.[19] Unfortunately, the application of these tests to cases involving insurance policies may prove somewhat problematic. In the common case where the contract is entered into after the policyholder has submitted an application and proposal form, English law at least is far from clear on the question of when and where the contract comes into existence. What is clear is that the proposal form is at most an offer of a contract (since the insurer is still at liberty to decline the proposal) so the submission of the proposal form does not by itself create a contract. The acceptance of the offer must then come from the insurer, and it is only on the happening of this acceptance and its communication to the proposer that there can be a contract. However, the decision to accept the proposal will normally be made in the insurer's office. These need not give rise to problems where the insurer's office is in the same State as that where the policyholder has his habitual residence, but it will surely be relatively uncommon for a policyholder and an insurer in the same State to be insuring a risk situated in another State, given the definition of the situation of the risk explained above. Much more commonly the parties will be in different States and the risk will be situated in one of those States. Given that the acceptance is made in the insurer's office, it seems that many contracts in this category will be made in the insurer's State rather than in the policyholder's State; thus, in the absence of an express choice of law, the applicable law is again likely to be the insurer's law. This tendency is reinforced by the fact that any express choice of law clause is much more likely to nominate the insurer's law than the policyholder's law. In some legal systems it might be possible to circumvent this result by arguing that the acceptance does not take effect until received, so that it takes place in the policyholder's State. English law is of course unable to adopt this convenient solution because of its rule that an acceptance made by post takes effect when posted.[20] So far as arbitration is concerned, there may or may not be an arbitration clause. Paragraph (h) tries to resolve some of these difficulties by providing that the contract is rebuttably presumed to be most closely

---

18   *R v International Trustee for the Protection of Bondholders A/G* [1937] A.C. 500.
19   *Vita Food Products Inc v Unus Shipping Co*, above.
20   *Adams v Lindsell* (1818) 1 B & Ald 681.

connected with the Member State in which the risk is situated. Unfortunately, paragraph (h) gives no indication of what evidence will be sufficient to rebut that presumption. In English law the general rule about presumptions is that they apply only so long as there is no evidence at all; once there is evidence, the presumption disappears and the matter must be decided according to the evidence.[21]

In the end it appears that these provisions of the Directive add little to the general private international law rule that the court must decide what is the proper law of the contract, either by applying some (often fairly notional) idea of the intentions of the parties or by deciding what would be the fairest solution.

Paragraph (c) of art. 7.1 extends the freedom given in the previous paragraph. It applies where the policyholder pursues a commercial or industrial activity or a liberal profession and where the contract covers two or more risks relating to those activities and situated in different Member States. In this situation the parties may choose the law of any of the Member States where an insured risk is situated or the law of the Member State where the policyholder has his habitual residence. Paragraph (h), discussed above, is again applicable in cases where the policy contains no express choice of law clause.

Both these paragraphs also raise the question of the validity of express choice of law clauses which purport to choose a legal system other than those which they authorise. Paragraph (d) of art. 7.1 attempts to deal with this situation by providing that where the Member States referred to in those paragraphs grant greater freedom of choice of applicable law, the parties may take advantage of that freedom. Unfortunately, this is another paragraph which raises as many questions as it answers. By definition this question arises only where there is more than one Member State whose law could conceivably apply to the situation. If the laws of all the Member States concerned allow the parties greater freedom of choice, then it is clear that paragraph (d) applies, but what is the situation if the laws of only some of the Member States concerned allow this freedom? The reference to the laws 'of *the* Member States' seems to imply that all relevant Member States must permit this freedom if it is to be available to the parties. It is submitted, however, that this is not the correct interpretation. It is sufficient if the law of any of the Member States referred to in the two paragraphs permits a wider choice of law, for in that event the parties can then effectively choose the law of that Member State and then take advantage of the freedom which it grants. It is submitted that this interpretation is the most appropriate one to give effect to the apparently liberal intentions of this part of art. 7, even though it

---

21   Though the force of that evidence is obviously extremely important.

may at first sight appear to run contrary to the English law principle that the doctrine of *renvoi* does not apply in contractual cases.[22] In fact this is not an attempt to apply *renvoi*, since that doctrine refers to the mandatory reference from one legal system to another in cases where private international law initially assigns the case to one legal system rather than to the case where the parties expressly and freely choose a particular legal system to govern their legal relations.

Paragraph (h) also contains an important exception applicable where one severable part of a contract has a close connection with a Member State other than that applicable to the rest of the contract. In such a case that severable part may by way of exception be governed by the law of the State with which it has the closest connection. It is suggested, however, that there will be very few cases falling into this category, given the two requirements which must be fulfilled – part of the contract must be severable, a relatively rare phenomenon in itself, and that part must have its closest connection with a Member State other than the one with which the rest of the contract is most closely connected.

Paragraph (i) then deals with the problems arising in States which are made up of a number of territorial units each having its own rules for contractual obligations. These rules are of course of relevance in the context of the United Kingdom, where Scotland does have its own law of contract. For the purposes of art. 7 each territorial unit within a Member State is considered a separate country for the purposes of identifying the applicable law. This simply means that, for example, a contract made in Scotland between a Scots policyholder and a Scots insurer will be subject to Scots law, it being impossible in this context to speak of the law of the United Kingdom. However, paragraph (i) also provides that the provisions of art. 7 do not apply to resolving conflicts between different territorial units of the same Member State unless that Member State chooses to make them applicable.

Art. 7.2 reinforces the general rule that Member States may override the general principles of art. 7.1 by providing that in certain situations (determined by the law of the Member State) the application of the *lex fori* is mandatory, whatever law would otherwise have been applicable to the contract. Rules of this kind are normally imposed on grounds of public policy, and it is to be noted that they have nothing to do with any choice of law on the part of the parties to the contract.

The overall effect of art. 7 is thus to provide something of a gloss on the traditional choice of law rules applied in private international law. To the extent that the Directive rules differ from the ordinary English law rules, it

---

[22]   *Re United Railways of the Havana and Regla Warehouses Ltd* [1960] Chapter 52.

was therefore necessary to have implementing legislation to bring English law into line with the Directive. This was achieved through the Contracts (Applicable Law) Act 1990, which is discussed in Chapter 5.

Art. 5 of the Directive deals with the concept of 'large risks'. The definition of this concept is important because, as appears below, policyholders seeking cover for large risks are generally treated as being in less need of protection than those seeking cover for mass risks and the rules regarding the free provision of services to them are therefore more lax.

There are three groups of large risks which the Directive identifies, and in all three cases a vital consideration is the class of risk, using the classifications adopted for the purposes of the Annex to the First Directive. In the case of the second and third categories of large risk there are also other criteria.

The first group of large risks is those falling under classes 4 (damage to or loss of railway rolling stock), 5 (damage to or loss of aircraft), 6 (damage to or loss of river and canal vessels, lake and sea vessels), 7 (all damage to or loss of goods in transit or baggage, irrespective of the form of transport), 11 (all liability arising out of the use of aircraft, including carrier's liability) and 12 (all liability arising out of the use of ships, vessels or boats on the seas, lakes, rivers or canals, including carrier's liability) of point A in the Annex. These risks are large risks without reference to the characteristics of the policyholder.

The second group of large risks is those falling under classes 14 (insolvency–general, export credit, instalment credit, mortgages, agricultural credit) and 15 (direct and indirect suretyship) of point A of the Annex. However, these are large risks only where the policyholder is engaged professionally in an industrial or commercial activity or in one of the liberal professions and the risks relate to such activity.

The third group of large risks is those falling under points 8 (damage to or loss of property through fire and natural forces), 9 (damage to or loss of property due to hail or frost and any event such as theft, other than those falling under point 8), 13 (all liability claims other than those falling under points 10, 11 and 12) and 16 (miscellaneous financial loss) of point A of the Annex. These risks are large risks only where the policyholder meets at least two of the following three criteria:[23]

(i)   balance sheet total 6.2 million ECU;
(ii)   net turnover 12.8 million ECU;
(iii) average number of employees during the financial year 250.

---

[23]   The criteria in this form apply from 1 January 1993; prior to that date the figures were approximately twice their present level.

These definitions of mass risk are relevant to the question of choice of law, since art. 7.1(f) provides that in the case of large risks the parties to the contract are free to choose any law as the applicable law, though it is to be assumed that, as in other cases under art. 7 an express choice can be over-ridden on grounds of public policy or because the law of the Member State requires the adoption of the *lex fori*.

The definition of large risk is relevant also to the freedom to provide services, though the provisions on this subject contained in the Second Directive have now been repealed and replaced by provisions in the Third Directive.

Art. 8 of the Directive deals with contracts for compulsory insurance, ie those cases, such as motor insurance, where the law of a Member State forbids the carrying on of any activity without an appropriate insurance policy. The article allows the offering and concluding of compulsory contracts in accordance with the First and Second Directives. A problem which may arise is that the law of the Member State imposing the obligation and the law of the Member State where the risk is situated may conflict as to the requirements of an appropriate compulsory policy. In this event art. 8.3 makes the former law prevail. In order to make art. 8 practically workable, art. 8.5 requires each Member State to inform the Commission of the risks against which insurance is compulsory under its legislation, stating the specific legal provision relating to that insurance and the particulars which must be given in the certificate which an insurer must issue to an insured person where that State requires proof that the obligation to take out insurance has been complied with. A Member State may require that those particulars include a declaration by the insurer to the effect that the contract complies with the specific provisions relating to that insurance. Where a certificate is issued which conforms with these requirements, a Member State must accept it as proof that the insurance obligation has been fulfilled.

When Member States have notified the Commission in the above terms, the Commission must publish the particulars supplied in the Official Journal.

Art. 12 of the Directive applies where an undertaking, through an establishment situated in a Member State covers a risk situated in another Member State. The latter State shall be the State of provision of services.

Under art. 14 of the Directive an undertaking which intends to carry on business for the first time in one or more Member States under the freedom to provide services must first inform the authorities of its home Member State, indicating the nature of the risks it proposes to cover. This requirement, inserted into the Second Directive by the Third Directive, accords with the general principle of home State regulation. Art. 16 goes on to stipulate how the home State authorities must respond to such a notification. The essence of art. 16 is that it provides for co–operation between the home State authorities and those of the other Member States where the insurer proposes to carry on business. Within one month of receiving a notification under art. 14 the authorities of the home State must inform the authorities of each Member State where the undertaking proposes to carry on business of the notification, providing a certificate that the undertaking has the necessary solvency margin, calculated in accordance with the provisions of the First Directive, discussed above, and stating the classes of risks which the undertaking has been authorised to cover and the nature of the risks which the undertaking proposes to cover in the Member State where it wishes to provide services. The same notification must be given to the undertaking concerned, which may start to provide the services as from the date of that notification. Art. 16.2 gives the authorities of the home State a residual right to refuse to provide this notification, thereby preventing the undertaking from starting to provide the services, but this refusal is subject to a right of appeal to the courts of the home State.

The same procedure of notification to the authorities of the home State followed by communication to the authorities of the other Member States concerned is also required if there is any change in the information provided under art. 14, ie the nature of the risks to be covered.[24]

Art. 12A of the Directive makes special provision for insurers offering motor insurance under the free provision of services. The particular difficulty which arises in this context is that every Member State is required[25] to operate a national bureau and guarantee fund along the lines of the United Kingdom's Motor Insurers Bureau, designed to ensure that there is compensation for the victims of road accidents caused by the negligence of a driver, even where that driver has failed to comply with the requirement to have an insurance policy in force. In each country this scheme is funded by a levy on all the motor insurers in that country. Clearly, it would not be acceptable for an insurer to provide motor insurance in a Member State on the basis of free provision of services without bearing an appropriate share of the costs of the levy for that State. Art. 12A therefore compels the Member State of provision of services to require all insurers providing motor insurance in its territory, whether established there or not, to become members of the bureau and guarantee fund and to contribute to the funding of the scheme. The undertaking is required to ensure that persons claiming in respect of risks in the State of provision of services are not in a worse position as a result of the fact that they have insured with an insurer who is not established in that State. For this purpose the Member State where the services are provided shall require the undertaking to appoint a resident

---

24 Art. 17.
25 Art. 12A.2.

representative to collect all information relating to claims and where necessary to represent the undertaking in the courts or before the authorities of the Member State where the services are provided in dealing with claims and with questions about the existence and validity of motor vehicle liability policies. On the other hand the contribution required to the guarantee fund must be calculated on the same basis for non–established insurers as for established insurers. Art. 26 of the Directive deals with co–insurance, and should be understood in the context of Directive 78/473,[26] under which a doubt had arisen as to the need for authorisation of the leading insurer and the co–insurer(s) in the State where the insurance is to be provided. Art. 26 resolves these doubts by providing that the lead insurer must either be regulated in the State where the risk is situated or must comply with the provisions discussed above as to the exercise of the right to provide services. By contrast, the co–insurer(s) need not meet either of these requirements.

Arts 28–35 of the Directive are the Final Provisions. Art. 28 mirrors the First Directive in calling on the Member States and the Commission to collaborate closely for the purpose of facilitating the supervision of direct insurance within the Community. It also requires Member States to inform the Commission of any major difficulties to which the application of the Directive gives rise. A particular concern to which art. 28 alludes is the risk that a Member State will suffer an abnormal transfer of insurance business to the detriment of undertakings established in its territory and to the advantage of branches and agencies located just beyond its borders. This situation is perhaps hard to imagine in the case of the United Kingdom, given its geographical position, but it could happen to other States more centrally located. If it did occur, it might be seen as evidence that the Member State suffering this transfer was perceived as having higher regulatory standards than its neighbours, so that insurers found it to their advantage to sell insurance in that territory without being fully subject to the regulatory standards normally applied there.[27] A simple way to achieve this would be to operate from a branch or agency just outside that territory.

Art. 28 also authorises the Commission to submit to the Council appropriate proposals for dealing with any problems which might arise. As yet it has not been necessary for the Commission to make use of these powers, though the current review of the Internal Market in Insurance, resulting from the Green Book of May 1996,[28] may lead to legislative proposals.

---

[26] Discussed later in this chapter at p. 59.
[27] For a more detailed consideration of the 'Race to the Bottom' see Chapter 4.
[28] A detailed account of the Green Book may be found in Chapter 7.

Art. 29 requires the Commission to forward to the Council regular reports on the development of the Market in Insurance transacted under the freedom to provide services.

In summary it can be seen that the Second Directives represent an important stage in the development of the Internal Market in Insurance. Although they do not by themselves create a complete Internal Market, since they do not allow an automatic right of establishment in other Member States for insurers authorised in one Member State, they do for the first time expressly open up the possibility that an insurer established and authorised in one Member State may by virtue of that authorisation be able to provide insurance services in another Member State.

The Second generation Directives are perhaps more difficult to evaluate than are their predecessors. These two Directives must clearly be set in the context of the 1992 Single Market Programme, of which they form part, both temporally and in intention. At the same time they are no more than an interim measure on the path to the Single Market, and the question must be asked, why take these measures at this time? The answer clearly lies in a conscious decision to prioritise the development of the freedom to provide services ahead of the right of establishment. This decision can be justified, not on the basis that freedom to provide services is more important than the right of establishment – it clearly is not – but on the pragmatic grounds that the legal issues to which it gives rise are simpler than those relating to the right of establishment. In particular, freedom to provide services can be achieved without imposing major additional duties on regulatory authorities, whereas realising the Single Passport System creates a need for considerable additional bureaucracy. Indeed, it is one of the most noticeable features of the Second generation Directives that they require little or nothing of the national regulatory authorities. From one point of view this might even be said to be a weakness of these Directives. They create various freedoms for insurers and policyholders, but do not address important questions about how the national regulatory authorities are to ensure that these freedoms are not abused. It appears to be assumed that home State regulation will operate, since there is no provision for insurers wishing to avail themselves of the freedom to provide services to notify the authorities of the host State of what they are doing. This is a logical arrangement, since it is inherent in the freedom to provide services that the service is provided from the home State (otherwise there would be an attempted exercise of the right of establishment) but the obvious danger is that policyholders in the State where the services are received will think that they are dealing under the regulatory arrangements obtaining in their home State and that the rules relating to the marketing and selling of the policy are those of the receiving State. It is not at all clear that this is the case, since these rules are not part of the proper law of the contract, not being terms of the contract. It might well be thought that the Second generation Directives are the least satisfactory of the three generations of Directives, principally because of their failure to integrate properly the regulatory and contractual issues. At the same time it might also be surmised that the Commission saw these Directives as no more than an interim measure on the way to the creation of the full Single Passport System. Such a view, while understandable, would also be unfortunate, for it appears likely that freedom to provide services will continue to be an important aspect of the insurance market even after the introduction of the Single Passport System. Provision of insurance on a services basis is always likely to be easier and cheaper than the creation of a permanent establishment, and the recent growth in the market for provision of insurance services by telephone only serves to emphasise this point. Once it becomes culturally acceptable to buy insurance by telephone (a process already well advanced in the United Kingdom) the arguments in favour of creating a permanent establishment in a foreign country are significantly weakened.

C.   3rd Generation

The Third generation of Directives[29] was designed to complete the Single Passport System, and the changes to which it led represented the most important development of the system of insurance regulation in the European Union since regulatory systems became commonplace in the 19th century. The Third generation put in place the system of home country regulation, the practical details of which are considered at length in the following Chapter, combining this system with a right of residual control for the authorities of host States.

The Second Life Directive[30] operates according to broadly similar principles, but it is necessary to draw attention to some important differences between the Life Directive and the non–Life Directive. Turning first to the recitals to this Directive, it can be seen that in the interval between the enactment of the Second non–Life Directive and the enactment of this Directive, the Commission's understanding of some of the issues relating to the Internal Market generally had developed. This is reflected in particular in the reference to the extent to which account needs to be taken of the differing levels of development of different economies within the EC and thus of the efforts which some Member States need to make in order to bring their economies into line with the general EC standard.

---

29   Directive 92/49 (non–Life); Directive 92/96 (Life).
30   Directive 90/619.

In the substantive provisions of the Directive four major points of difference may be noted between the Life Directive and the non–Life Directive. These concern the notion of the Member State of Commitment, the choice of law, rights of cancellation and the differing levels of protection afforded to different policyholders.

The Member State of the Commitment is the term used in place of the expression 'Member State where the risk is situated' in the non–Life Directive. It is defined by art. 2 of the Directive as meaning the Member State where the policyholder has his habitual residence.[31] Art. 4 then goes on to deal with choice of law questions. The presumption is always that the applicable law of a life policy is the law of the Member State of the Commitment. However, where the law of that State allows, the parties may choose another law. By art. 4.2 where the policyholder is a natural person and has his habitual residence in a Member State other than that of which he is a national, the parties may choose the law of the State of which he is a national. This rule appears to be unnecessary, since the general rule that the parties may choose the law which they prefer surely includes the possibility of making this choice, In any event, art. 4.4 makes clear that the general freedom to choose is subject to rules requiring the mandatory application of the *lex fori*.

Art. 15 of the Directive deals with rights of cancellation. There is of course no corresponding provision in the non–Life Directive, since it is not customary to allow rights of cancellation in non–Life policies. Art. 15 requires Member States to include in their law a provision giving policyholders a period of between 14 and 30 days in which to cancel a policy, the time to run from the date on which the policyholder is informed that the policy has been concluded. Where the policyholder gives notice of cancellation, this must have the effect of releasing him from any future obligation arising under the contract. It is important to note that the Directive says nothing about releasing the policyholder from past obligations or from the effect of transactions already executed. This is of great importance in dealing with investment policies, especially single–premium investment policies, where it is still possible for a policyholder to be exposed to the risk of a fall in the value of the fund between the execution of the policy and the exercise of the right of cancellation. These questions, as well as everything else relating to the conditions of cancellation are expressly left to be determined by the law of the Member State of the Commitment. The only permissible derogations from the general rules about the right of cancellation arise in relation to policies of a duration not exceeding six months and cases

---

[31] In the consideration of this Directive, as in that of the non–Life Directive, 'habitual residence' includes the place of establishment of a legal person.

where because of the status of the policyholder or the circumstances in which the contract is concluded, the policyholder does not need this special protection. The cases in this latter category are not further explained in the Directive, and the interpretation of the provision is therefore left to the Member States, subject to the right of the Commission to bring art. 169 proceedings alleging a failure to implement the Directive correctly.

D. Implementation

The First and Second generation Directives were implemented some years ago throughout the Member States. The implementation date for the Third generation of Directives was 1 July 1994, and this deadline was met by the majority of Member States. As at June 1996 the Third generation Directives had been implemented by all the Member States except for Greece. These Directives do not allow Greece any derogation as to the time limits, and it thus follows that Greece is in breach of its obligations under the TEU. By August 1996 no art. 169 proceedings had been commenced against Greece, though the failure to implement the Directives was obviously a matter of concern to the Commission, which was seeking to secure the correct implementation of the Directives without further delay.[32]

The Third generation Directives are intended to realise the vital final stage in the process of creating the Single Market. They make rational (perhaps inevitable) decisions about the regulatory structure to be adopted. What they of course cannot do is to create the necessary Market culture to make the Single Market a reality.

A proper evaluation of the approach adopted to date requires the development of some criteria by which existing legislation can be judged. At the simplest level it is possible to enquire how far the legislation goes in creating a Single Market in Insurance. From this point of view it would inevitably be judged that the project is more or less complete on the regulatory side (though questions remain about the regulation of marketing and selling practices, which are not as yet harmonised) though not on the contract law side. It is submitted, however, that such an approach is simplistic. The question is not simply whether *a* Single Market has been completed, but whether the best achievable Single Market has been created. The question is deliberately formulated in this limited way because it is clear that the ideal Single Market has not been and will not be created. Such a

---

[32]   *The Functioning of the System in Practice, Its Deficiencies and the Implications for Insurance Companies*, paper given by Maria Velentza of DGXV at EIPA conference on Community Law and the Insurance Sector, Luxembourg 17 June 1996.

Market would involve identity of laws throughout the Member States, coupled with a single regulatory authority. For reasons discussed in Chapter 8, this is not likely to happen at any time in the foreseeable future.

It can be seen that the Directives enacted and implemented to date have largely completed the process of establishing the regulatory framework for the Internal Market in Insurance, though this has been achieved at the cost of treating insurance as an area separate from other types of financial service, an approach whose problems are explored in Chapter 8.

E. Other Legislation

(i) Co–insurance

The Co–insurance Directive of 1978[33] was aimed at those Member States (of which the United Kingdom was not one) which forbade the insurance of a risk situated in their territory by an insurer not established there. The Directive requires national legislation to be amended so as to allow insurers established in other States to join as co–insurers of risks situated in their States. The leading insurer must be established in one of the Member States, but not necessarily in the State of the risk.[34] Because the law in the United Kingdom had never prohibited non–resident insurers from insuring risks in the UK, the Directive did not require substantial changes in the law in the UK. In *Commission v Germany*[35] it was held that this Directive does not justify a requirement that the leading insurer in a co–insurance contract must be established in the Member State where the risk is located.[36] In the same case it was said that co–insurance does not concern consumers, with the result that arguments based on consumer protection as a justification for restricting freedom to provide services have less force than they might have in other areas of insurance.

The limited freedom established by the Directive has now been superseded by the more general freedoms contained in the Second and Third generation Directives.

---

[33] Directive 78/473.
[34] Case 205/84 [1987] 2 CMLR 89.
[35] Case 205/84 above; and see Lasok (1988) 51 MLR 706.
[36] It was also held that such a requirement infringes arts 59 and 60 EEC; see Chapter 2.

(ii)   Third Party Liability

There are two Directives dealing with third party liability. They are Directive 84/5 and Directive 90/232. Both relate to the approximation of national laws on insurance against civil liability arising from the use of motor vehicles. The major effect of these Directives has been to extend the range of risks against which a motor insurance policy in the Member States is required to cover. Specifically, it is now compulsory to have cover against the risk of negligently caused damage to the property of others, whereas before these Directives the only requirement was for cover against the risk of negligently caused personal injury to others. The Directive thus represents a significant step in the direction of third party protection as compared with the former position. In the United Kingdom such changes as were necessary were implemented by the Road Traffic Act 1988.

(iii)   Credit Insurance and Suretyship Insurance

Directive 87/343 amends Directive 73/239 (the first non–Life Directive) in the particular context of credit insurance and suretyship insurance. Directive 73/239 had expressly contemplated[37] the need for further subsequent legislation, not least because that Directive had allowed Germany to maintain its prohibition on combining suretyship insurance with other classes of insurance. The Directive removes Germany's exemption in this respect, as well as making provision for equalisation reserves for credit insurance, together with a higher level of guarantee fund than is required in other classes of insurance. The Directive is of little general importance, being designed only to tidy up some anomalies and special problems arising in this specialised field.

(iv)   Legal Expenses Insurance

Directive 87/343 deals with the co–ordination of laws and procedures relating to legal expenses insurance. In so doing it takes up the idea of harmonising the law in the area of legal expenses insurance which was mentioned in art. 7(2)(c) of Directive 73/239 (the first non–Life Directive). The major purpose of this Directive was to address one specific problem which had arisen in those cases where legal expenses insurance was provided as an incidental part of another policy. The best-known example was in

---

[37]   Art 2(2)(d).

motor policies, where it was common to provide that the insurance covered the expenses of legal proceedings to establish liability. In such cases an insurer liable for the legal expenses as well as for any legal liability might have an incentive to refuse to agree that the case was sufficient to justify the bringing of proceedings, preferring instead to concede liability, thereby damaging the policyholder's no–claims discount. In order to address this problem Directive 87/343 imposes a requirement that the legal expenses insurance be provided by a different insurers than the one providing the rest of the cover under the policy, though it is still permitted to have both aspects of cover expressed as falling within a single policy.

Before the implementation of this Directive Germany had had a rule which required insurers providing legal expenses insurance to specialise in that activity to the exclusion of any other form of insurance. The justification for this rule was said to be that insurers providing both legal expenses insurance and insurance against the risk which might be the subject matter of litigation would have a potential conflict of interest in that in doubtful cases it might be to their financial advantage to admit liability for a modest sum rather than fighting the case. Where, as in motor insurance, it is usual to visit an increased premium upon a policyholder as the consequence of a successful claim, the insurer would then protect itself by levying the higher premium the following year. The policyholder would naturally have preferred the case to be fought. As the recitals to the Directive admit, the German system did effectively preclude the conflicts of interest at which the Directive was aimed; however, the method appeared disproportionate to the aim pursued, and a decision to extend this system to the other Member States would have required the breaking–up of a number of composite undertakings which had for a long time provided both legal expenses cover and other forms of insurance. It was therefore decided that the preferable approach would be to require Germany to abolish its specialisation rule rather than to extend it to the remaining Member States.

F.   Summary

The legislation in areas other than regulation displays no conceptual coherence and discloses no overall plan. The Commission's approach has been to tidy up individual problems as they have appeared. The original proposal for a wide–ranging insurance contract law Directive[38] has been abandoned and seems unlikely to be resurrected in the foreseeable future.

---

[38]   OJ C190/2 28.7.79; see Chapter 5.

G.   Conclusion

When the history of insurance legislation at EU level is considered as a whole, it appears that the overriding feature of the Commission's approach has been pragmatism. The several steps in creating the necessary regulatory apparatus have been taken when circumstances permitted and in the ways which seemed most practicable at the time. Although the interim positions achieved by this approach have sometimes looked rather difficult to defend (especially after the Second generation Directives) the overall effect by 1997 can be seen to be a structure which achieves most of what is realistically achievable at the present time. Related questions to be considered in later Chapters include the more detailed issues surrounding the system of home country control[39] and the possibility that a Fourth generation of Directives may yet be needed to resolve some remaining problems.[40]

On the contract side there is little to be said. The Commission has identified a number of largely unrelated problems, some having to do with issues of consumer protection, others being related to structural and technical issues within the insurance market. These have been resolved on an *ad hoc* basis. At present there are no plans for further Directives in this area. For the future, either there is to be a general harmonisation of European private law (apparently unlikely at present) in which case insurance will no doubt be included, or there is not, in which case insurance contract law will remain largely as it is.

---

[39]   Chapter 4.
[40]   Chapter 8.

4 The System of Home Country Regulation

In deciding what techniques of supervision were to be applied to insurance undertakings operating across national borders under the Single Passport system a fundamental choice had to be made between regulation by the home State of the undertaking concerned and regulation by the host State in which the undertaking operates. On the face of it the latter option might well have seemed attractive, particularly to individual Member States concerned about the regulatory standards and practices prevailing elsewhere in the EU. A system of host country regulation would have allowed each national market to be a self-contained system within which consistent standards would have been applied. By contrast, a system of home country regulation leads inevitably to the position that two or more undertakings operating in the same Member State may have different regulators and may therefore in practice be subject to different standards and practices.

Despite the superficial attractions of host country regulation, it is reasonably clear that a serious pursuit of the Single European Market requires the adoption of a system of home country regulation, coupled with measures to ensure that there is the greatest possible degree of uniformity in the standards applied in different Member States. The reasons for this may be simply stated. Host country regulation is a recipe for the continuing partition of the Market along national lines; it is by its nature inimical to the kind of international inter–penetration of markets which is essential in order to create a true Single European Market. Moreover, it is administratively highly inefficient, since it would leave insurers needing a separate authorisation for each Member State in which they wished to transact business, presently a maximum of fifteen, though this number is likely to increase before the end of the century.

1. CO–ORDINATION BETWEEN NATIONAL AUTHORITIES

Clearly, an effective system of home country regulation, ie one which is to succeed in delivering appropriate levels of consumer protection, needs a reasonable degree of collaboration and co–ordination between the regulatory authorities of the different Member States, for it is practically impossible for the authorities of any one State to monitor effectively what is done in other States by those insurers which it has authorised.

This fact may be seen as highlighting a serious difficulty in the present approach to the regulation of insurance business. Although a system of pure host country regulation is unworkable for the reasons given above, it is equally clear that a system of pure home country regulation, while better than host country regulation, is also significantly defective. The problem which this exemplifies is in reality a microcosm of the most fundamental problem of the whole Internal Market Programme, namely that there can be no true Internal Market until the regulatory and other rules are identical throughout the European Union. Only then will it truly be possible to say that business between London and Madrid or Milan is as easy as business between London and Manchester. Equally, it is clear that this uniformity of laws, even at the regulatory level, is not going to be achieved so long as the details of day–to–day regulation are delegated to national authorities. The only way to achieve the necessary uniformity is to centralise the regulatory process. In its simplest version this would involve a single regulatory authority, presumably situated in Brussels, where all decisions would be made. In practical terms the argument is that regulation should be handed over to the Commission as part of its task of monitoring and developing the Internal Market. It would of course be possible for the Commission to establish offices in each Member State as a way of facilitating the administration of the regulatory system and improving contacts with individual insurers, though it would have to be clearly stipulated that these offices acted on behalf of the Commission, rather than on behalf of any national authority.

In the context of insurance, and perhaps of financial services more generally, the prospect of such centralisation of the regulatory process may not give rise to great alarm. The underlying difficulty is that the logic of the argument in relation to financial services appears to apply with equal force to other areas of business activity. Once this is realised, it can be seen that the proposal is in its long–term effects a proposal for a very substantial transfer of power away from national regulatory authorities and to the Commission – a move of power to the centre, in other words. Whatever the administrative merits of this argument (and it is submitted that they are considerable) it seems unlikely that the logic of the argument will prevail at a time when the whole Internal Market Programme appears to be in danger of falling victim to a rising trend of Europhobia in at least some of the Member States. A question to be considered in more detail in the final Chapter is how the rational development of the Internal Market can best be pursued in a rather hostile climate of this kind.

A. Residual Rights of the Host State

When considering the development of the Single Market in Insurance, it must be borne in mind that the system of home country regulation does not mean that host States have no rights or responsibilities at all in relation to the supervision of insurers from other Member States providing services within their territory. In particular, host State authorities have a residual power to impose conditions on the exercise of the freedom to provide services and the right of establishment, based on the somewhat nebulous concept of the 'general good'.

B. The General Good – ECJ Case Law[1]

An important qualification to the general principles of freedom to provide services is found in the rule contained in the Third Directives[2] which allows Member States to derogate from the freedom of establishment or to impose other restrictions in the 'general good'. This expression is not further defined in the Directives, but has in a more general context been the subject of consideration by the Court of Justice. In simple terms it may be said that the concept of the general good allows Member States, in areas where the law has not been harmonised, to maintain certain national measures even though these have the effect of derogating from the general principles of free movement which underlie the Single Market. The 'general good' is capable of being used in relation to derogations from any of the Four Freedoms, though in the present context the focus will naturally be on its application to services and in particular to financial services. As was explained in Chapter 2, arts 52–59 TEU are directly applicable, and directly discriminatory national rules must be brought within arts 55–56 if they are to be justified. Non-discriminatory national rules which nevertheless derogate from the principles of the Single Market may be justified if they meet the following criteria:

> The measure must apply indistinctly to all service providers in the sector in question, whatever their nationality and wherever they are established (the non–discrimination test);

---

1 For a good account of the problems in this area see C. van Schoubreck, *The Concept of the General Good*, in McGee and Heusel (eds), *The Law and Practice of Insurance in the Single European Market* (1994) Bundesanzeiger.

2 Art. 32.4 in both the Life and non–Life Directives; the concept also appears in the Second Credit Institutions Directive, Directive 89/646 of 15 December 1989 OJ L386 30.12.89.

The restrictions on the freedom to provide services must be justified by very strong reasons of public interest. Consumer protection is commonly cited as the most obvious of these reasons, though it need not be the only one. Certainly it is the one most likely to be of relevance in an insurance context (the public interest test);

The public interest in question must not yet be protected by rules imposed on foreign service providers in the Member State where they are established. In other words, the host country is not justified in imposing requirements which merely duplicate those imposed by the service providers' home country (the non–duplication test);

The restriction must be no more than is reasonably necessary to achieve the legitimate objectives being pursued. If the same end could be achieved by a less restrictive scheme of regulation, then that scheme should be adopted in place of the existing one (the proportionality test).

It is important to understand that this concept originated in the case law of the Court of Justice[3] rather than in Directives. Thus, it was developed in relation to areas, notably, free movement of goods,[4] where the relevant legislation contained no mention of the 'general good' and gave no indication that there could be any derogation of this kind from the general Single Market principles.[5] A brief account of the major cases decided by the ECJ in this area may be helpful. In *Schindler*[6] it was said that restrictions on playing the lottery in another Member State, although obviously a *prima facie* restraint on trade, might be justified if they were for the protection of consumers and for the maintenance of order in society. Such an argument

---

3   The most important cases include *Commission v Germany* 4/12/86 – Consumer Protection.

Alpine Investments BV – Case C384/93 Protection of good reputation of national financial sector.

Schindler – Case C275/92 Social Order and Prevention of Fraud.

Coditel – Case 62/70 [1980] ECR 881 – Protection of Intellectual Property.

Commission v Italy – Case C180/89 [1991] ECR 709 – Protection of national artistic heritage.

Bachmann – [1992] ECR 249 – Cohesion of tax system.

Johannes Gerritt – Case 55/93 5/10/92 – Road Safety.

4   Early cases include *Dassonville, van Binsbergen* and *Reynders.*

5   Dubuisson, B., *Unité ou diversité de notions d'intérêt général, d'ordre publique et des normes impératives dans les directives communautaires relatives aux assurances*, in L'Europe de l'assurance. Les directives de la troisième génération Maklu Uitgevers 1992.

6   Above, note 3.

presumably rests on a fear that participation in gambling of this kind will prove addictive, and that this in turn will lead to poverty and financial hardship. It would therefore seem difficult at the present day to sustain this argument in any Member State which has its own lottery, and this may be regarded as an example of the general point that the use of the 'general good' as a ground for restricting the freedom to provide services must be restricted to indistinctly applicable measures.

In *van Schenk* the rule in issue was one which required garages authorised to carry out MOT tests on cars to be situated within the territory to which the Certificate related. This obviously restricted cross–border trade, since it meant that garages in other Member States could not offer this service. It was held that the importance of maintaining road safety was sufficient justification for this rule. It is suggested that this decision can be justified only on the basis that different Member States have significantly different rules for their MOT tests, and that the difficulties which the regulatory authorities of each State would experience in monitoring the activities of garages in other States meant that there could not be sufficient assurance of quality control. These propositions seem somewhat questionable: it is by no means clear that different States have radically different rules, and in reality it seems likely that cross–border services of this kind would be offered almost exclusively by those in border regions, so that the burden of monitoring placed on national regulatory authorities would not be excessive. In the present context the importance of the case is perhaps its recognition that different national standards may be a sufficient justification for restricting cross–border services. From an insurance point of view this may be equated to the situation where the domestic law of a Member State forbids or restricts the offering of a particular type of policy. The *van Schenk* principle might then be used to justify the authorities of the host State in imposing the same restrictions of an insurer from another Member State.

In Case C180/89 by contrast, the ECJ struck down a restrictive rule despite an attempt to invoke the 'general good' defence. The rule in question required that those acting as tourist guides in Italy have an Italian qualification for that job – foreign qualifications were not accepted. The justification advanced for this rule was that the Italian State wanted to ensure a sufficient degree of knowledge among tourist guides so that Italian history and culture were not misrepresented. The ECJ did not seek to dispute the legitimacy of the objective pursued, but took the view that the solution adopted was disproportionate in the absence of evidence that guide's from other Member States were in fact unable to provide the service to an adequate standard. The specifically cultural dimension to this case makes it difficult to draw from it any conclusions which would be relevant in the present context.

The final group of three cases in this area all have specific insurance law aspects. In *Bachman* the rule in issue was that contributions paid for sickness or invalidity insurance, or for pension or life assurance schemes were to be tax deductible only if the provider to whom they were paid was resident in the same State as the policyholder. This was an obvious disincentive to buying these products across borders, but the ECJ nevertheless held that the restriction could be justified on the basis that it contributed to maintaining the integrity of the national tax system. This apparently refers to the fact that the contributions on which tax relief is allowed will eventually form part of the income of the insurer and can be taken into account for tax purposes then, so long as the insurer is in the same State as the policyholder – if this requirement were not satisfied, the result would be tax relief in one State but taxation in another State, which would amount to a tax subsidy from one State to another. Unfortunately, the logical ramifications of this decision are absurd, for the same result occurs in any case where a business incurs a deductible expense by buying goods or services from another Member State, yet it is clear that a blanket restriction on such transactions could not possibly be justified. It might be possible to distinguish the general business expense case from that where individuals pay contributions to a state–administered fund, but that was not the position in *Bachman*. It is hard to see how this decision can possibly be sustained even at the time it was made, in view of the considerable progress since made in the development of the Single Market. Including the beginnings of progress towards the creation of a harmonised taxation system, the decision seems entirely outdated at the present day.

In Case 205/84, which was decided after the coming into force of the First generation Directives but before any subsequent harmonisation of the insurance market, the ECJ held that issues relating to the levels of technical reserves held by an insurer could possibly justify a 'General good' derogation from freedom to provide services. It seems that this decision must now be regarded as obsolete in view of the subsequent harmonisation of the rules relating to technical reserves.[7]

In Case 38/93 the ECH had to consider a ban in Dutch law on cold calling in an effort to sell insurance products. The ban, which was indistinctly applicable and designed to protect consumers from suffering undue pressure to buy, was upheld. This is an obvious and relatively straightforward example of the acceptance of consumer protection legislation as falling within the 'general good' exception.

However, when the Commission came to turn the principles of arts 52–66 into reality by means of specialised Directives, it chose in a number of

---

7   Art. 21.

sectors,[8] including insurance, to make express mention of the concept of the 'general good' as a ground for derogation from the general freedom to provide services. The principles developed in the earlier cases must therefore be assumed to have been incorporated into this sector by that reference.

This in turn leads to the question of how these principles are to be applied in an insurance context and, to turn the question into a more practical one, what kinds of derogations from the general freedom to provide services are likely to be accepted by the Court of Justice as being justified in the case of insurance. There is as yet no case law directly on the point, and educated speculation is the best that can be hoped for.

No Member State has attempted to produce a list, exhaustive or otherwise, of provisions in its own laws which it regards as inconsistent with the general freedoms but justified under this exemption. This is perhaps not surprising. It seems likely that most Member States will not have attempted to identify rules falling into this category. In so far as any Member State has identified rules likely to fall into this category, it would probably prefer to protect its tactical position by not admitting openly that these rules require to be justified under the 'general good' exemption. Should the question arise before the Court of Justice, the Member State would no doubt prefer to be in a position still to argue that the rules in question are not incompatible with arts 52–66, using the 'general good' only as a fallback position.

On the other hand the Directives do impose on the insurance authorities of Member States a duty to notify their counterparts in other Member States of restrictions which they intend to impose on insurers from other Member States on the basis of the 'general good'.[9]

It is clear that this derogation is capable of being used by Member States as a thinly disguised tool for preventing the entry of foreign insurers into the national market place. It is submitted that there is a fundamental difficulty about the use of the 'general good' exception, which will apply to a great many of the cases where it might possibly be used. An objection on the ground of the 'general good' must be taken either to a particular insurer or to a particular product or products or to particular selling practices as in Case 38/93. Where the objection is to an insurer, that insurer will by definition have been approved by the regulatory authorities of another Member State as satisfying the tests laid down in the national law (substantially harmonised under the provisions of the First generation Directives)[10] and it seems

---

8   For other good examples see the Banking co–ordination Directives – the First Directive, 77/780 of 12 December 1977 OJ L322 17.12.77, the Second Directive, 89/646 of 15 December 1989 OJ L386 30.12.89.

9   Art. 32.4 of both the Third Life and Third non–Life Directives.

10 See Chapter 1.

incompatible with the most basic notions of mutual recognition to challenge decisions of this kind taken in another Member State. Where the objection is to a product similar issues arise. Given that most Member States (though not the United Kingdom) operate systems for the prior approval of policies, and that even in the United Kingdom policies which are thought to be objectionable for some reason are likely to be withdrawn under pressure from the national regulatory authorities,[11] there is again an incongruity in objecting to policies which are accepted in the home State of the insurer. Of course it might happen that a particular policy was issued which was thought to give rise to legitimate concern, but in these circumstances the proper response is to raise the matter with the regulators in the home State and invite them to take action, rather than unilaterally prohibiting the policy in one of the Member States. Only where, as in Case 38/93, the objection is to a particular selling practice (and the measure is indistinctly applicable) can the rule realistically be thought to have any application in the insurance context. The earlier cases mentioned above might be thought to give rise to considerable difficulties in the current state of the Single Market. The logic of many of those decisions has already been questioned.[12] It is suggested that they reflect not a logical development of exceptions to the Four Freedoms, but rather an ill-considered attempt by the ECJ to develop, on a piecemeal basis, some category of cases where national sensitivities are such that the principles reflected in the Treaty cannot for political reasons be fully accepted. This rather cynical view of the case law may point simultaneously to two conclusions about likely future developments. The first is that the 'general good' exception ought to be very severely restricted, whilst the second is that in practice the cases where it is permitted are likely to be more numerous than they ought to be and are unlikely to fit any coherent pattern.

C.   Distance Selling

A particular feature of insurance is that it can in some circumstances be sold at a distance, ie without the need for any direct contact between the insurer and the policyholder. This may happen where a policy is sold 'off the page', ie by means of a newspaper (or even a broadcast) advertisement. Alternatively it may happen as the result of telephone conversations between

---

[11]   As happened, for example, in the case of policies which offered to provide chauffeurs for drivers disqualified as a result of failing breath tests, though these had been held not to be policies of insurance at all – see *DTI v St Christopher's Motorists' Association* [1974] 1 All E.R. 395.

[12]   See above.

the parties (or their agents). In some cases these conversations may have been initiated by the insurer 'cold–calling' prospective policyholders who have not expressed any interest in buying policies and who have not asked for or consented to the approach by the insurer.

Although insurance may be particularly prone to this form of selling, it is not the only service which can be sold in this way, and the EC has long recognised the consumer protection issues to which distance selling gives rise. There is a draft Distance Selling Directive,[13] though in its present form this does not cover the selling of financial services. The exclusion of financial services from the draft was a matter of some controversy. It is clear that distance selling does need to be regulated, partly because of its specific cross–border aspects, but also because of the enormous potential for abusive behaviour on the part of sellers. The question is what form that regulation is to take and whether it is to be applied indiscriminately to all sectors of business. The Second Directives deal with the selling of insurance on a services basis, but do not contain any provision relating to the problems of distance selling described in the previous paragraph. The general issue of balancing the commercial freedom to market one's products against the need to protect consumers from overly aggressive selling practices is one which goes well beyond the subject of insurance law, though the established tendency of some insurers towards aggressive marketing may well make the question one of particular importance in an insurance context. It is suggested that any general distance selling Directive which might be enacted needs to take particular account of the suitability (or unsuitability) of particular types of products for selling by this method, and should apply to sensibly discriminatory regimes accordingly.

D. The Third Directives

In the light of the foregoing discussion of the general issues it is now possible to consider in detail the provisions of the Third generation of Directives, which seek to implement the system of home country regulation. As with the earlier consideration of the First and Second generations of Directives, attention will be focused primarily on the non–Life Directive, with appropriate references to differences occurring in the Life Directive.

The Third Directives seek to complete the Internal Market from the point of view of both freedom to provide services and right of establishment. The third recital to the Directive is a reminder that the Second Directives largely created an Internal Market for commercial policyholders especially in

---

[13] OJ C288 30.10.95.

relation to large risks, but that this Internal Market did not extend to other policyholders or categories of risks. Recital 18 makes the assertion that the harmonisation of insurance contract law is not a prior condition for the achievement of the Internal Market in Insurance, with the result that sufficient protection will be given to policyholders by a rule allowing Member States to impose the application of their law to insurance contracts covering situations within their territories. It will be argued in the next Chapter that the premise underlying this recital is in fact wrong, and that it is necessary to harmonise insurance contract law in order to create a true Internal Market. Be that as it may, it is interesting to observe that the Commission clearly sees the residual right to impose a Member State's own law on particular contracts as the best alternative to the harmonisation of insurance contract law which is generally accepted as being politically and technically impracticable for the foreseeable future.

The early substantive arts of the Directive lay down the general provisions for obtaining authorisation. As these articles replace the original terms of the First Directive about the obtaining of authorisation, they have already been dealt with in the previous Chapter, where that Directive was extensively considered.

The provisions in the Third Directive which are entirely new and which therefore require further consideration are the following:

Art. 15 requires any natural or legal person who proposes to acquire directly or indirectly, a qualifying holding[14] in an insurance undertaking first to inform the authorities of the home Member State, indicating the size of his intended holding. There is a similar notification requirement if the holding of such a person is to be increased above 20%, 33% or 50%. The authorities of the home State then have three months in which to consider whether to oppose this plan, which they may do if they consider that the proposed shareholder is unsuitable in view of the need to ensure sound and prudent management of the undertaking in question. If they decide not to oppose the acquisition, they may set a maximum period for its implementation. There are similar notification requirements imposed on any shareholder who proposes to dispose of a qualifying holding in an insurance company, or to reduce his holding below any of the key thresholds of 50%, 33% or 20%, though the article does not give the home State authorities any power to raise objections to the disposal. Art. 15.3 supplements these obligations on shareholders by requiring insurers themselves to notify any such acquisitions or disposals which come to their notice, as well as, in any event, notifying the authorities once a year of all qualifying holdings in their shares of which they

---

14   Ie at least 10% of the shares or such a holding as would make it possible for him to exert a significant influence over the management of the undertaking concerned.

are aware (and they should be aware of all such holdings from an examination of their share register, since the domestic laws of Member States should contain provisions for compulsory notification to the company by any individual or group which acquires holdings in the company's shares of amounts significantly smaller than these thresholds).

Art. 15.4 deals with the consequences of non–compliance with the notification obligations imposed by 15.1 and 15.2, as well as with the more general problem of the holding of shares by persons whose influence on the undertaking is likely to operate against the sound and prudent management of the undertaking. Members States are required to introduce into their law an obligation for the competent regulatory authorities in these circumstances to take appropriate action to put an end to this situation. This action may include injunctions, sanctions against managers or directors or suspension of the exercise of the voting rights attaching to the shares held by the shareholders in question. Where shares are acquired despite the opposition of the competent authorities of the home State, the laws of the Member States must, at a minimum, provide for the exercise of the corresponding voting rights to be suspended, or for the nullity of the votes cast or for the possibility of their annulment.[15]

Art. 16 deals with the confidentiality of information received by competent authorities as part of their supervisory duties. Member States must provide that all information received under these circumstances is to be treated as confidential. The consequence of this is declared to be that no such information may be disclosed to anyone, except in summary or aggregate form (ie as it relates to regulated undertakings collectively) such that individual undertakings cannot be identified. However, this prohibition does not apply in cases covered by criminal law, so information may be disclosed to prosecuting authorities (or, presumably to the defence) for the purposes of evidence in a criminal trial. A more general exception to the confidentiality principle contained in art. 16.1 arises where an insurance undertaking has been declared bankrupt or is being compulsorily wound up. In these circumstances confidential information which does not concern third parties involved in trying to rescue the undertaking may be disclosed in civil as well as in criminal proceedings.

Art. 16.2 deals with exchange of information between the competent authorities of Member States. It provides that art. 16.1 is not to apply to exchanges of information in accordance with the Insurance Directives. It will be recalled that in a number of places these call for collaboration between the authorities of the various Member States. However, information received by the authorities of one Member State from those of another Member State is

---

[15]   Insurance Companies Act 1982 ss 61A–61B.

itself subject to the same obligations of confidentiality as are imposed by art. 16.1. Thus art. 16.4 further provides that authorities receiving information under arts 16.1 or 16.2 may only use it in the course of their duties to check that the conditions governing the taking up of the business of insurance are met, and to facilitate monitoring of the conduct of such business, to impose sanctions, in administrative appeals against the decisions of the competent authorities or in court proceedings initiated under art. 56[16] or under special provisions contained in the Insurance Directives. The restrictions on disclosure already mentioned do not preclude exchanges of information between two or more competent authorities in the same State or between Member States or in the discharge of their supervisory function between competent authorities and; authorities responsible for the supervision of credit institutions and other financial organisations and the authorities responsible for the supervision of financial markets; bodies involved in the liquidation and bankruptcy of insurance undertakings and in other similar procedures; persons responsible for carrying out statutory audits of the accounts of insurance undertakings and other financial institutions. Competent authorities may also disclose to bodies which administer compulsory winding–up proceedings or guarantee funds information necessary to the performance of their duties.

Member States are authorised by art. 16.6 to allow disclosure of certain information to other departments of their central government administrations responsible for legislation on the supervision of credit institutions, financial institutions, investment services and insurance companies and to inspectors acting on behalf of those departments.

An important protection for the confidentiality of information passed between different regulatory and supervisory bodies under the provisions of art. 16 is that Member States must provide that the further disclosure of such information is always subject to the prior consent of the competent authority from which it first came.

Art. 21 deals with the covering of technical provisions and lists exhaustively the categories of assets with which Member States may authorise insurers to cover their technical provisions. An important qualification to this list is contained in art. 21.1, which authorises Member States to impose more restrictive rules, under which not all assets of the categories listed in the Directive will be accepted for covering purposes. Art. 21.1 goes on to set out a series of principles which Member States must apply in their legislation relating to the covering of technical provisions. These are essentially accounting principles designed to ensure that the matching of assets is done on a sound and prudent basis.

---

16   For art. 56 see Chapter 2.

For the most part these provisions may be regarded as doing little more than supplementing existing national company law legislation, though they do to a limited extent give the insurance regulatory authorities a wider range of discretion and power to seek information than would arise under ordinary company law. The question of control over transfers of ownership of an insurance undertaking is not directly related to the development of the Single Market, since the powers given to the authorities in this regard apply irrespective of the residence of the person(s) acquiring control. On the other hand, it would not be surprising if the prospect of the transfer of control to a non–national were in practice seen as giving rise to particular problems. This is a potential source of controversy, since blatant discrimination on national lines in this regard would obviously violate the Single Market principle.

E. Conclusion

The adoption of a system of home country regulation was inevitable, for reasons given at the start of this Chapter. On the other hand, the use of a system in which control is vested at national level rather than at supranational level leaves a number of difficult areas of overlap and tension between different national regulatory authorities. The compromises in terms of information sharing and derogations from freedom to provide services and right of establishment contained in the Third Directives are an attempt to reconcile these conflicts. Given that the Directives are expressed as authorising refusal of authority only on the ground that the proposed acquirer is not a fit and proper person, it would seem that domestic laws could not legitimately allow for refusal on other grounds. To the extent that they did so, there would be a failure on the part of the Member State concerned to implement the Directive correctly, which might be the subject of proceedings under art. 169 TEU.

Even three years after the date for implementation of the Third Directives it is too early to say with any conviction how effective the various compromises have been. To date it does not appear that these provisions have given rise to major difficulties, however.

5 Insurance Contract Law

This chapter deals with issues relating to the law and practice of insurance contracts in the context of the attempt to develop a Single Market in Insurance. Four major areas are considered. Private International Law deals with the conflicts between two legal systems which arise when any cross-border insurance contract is made. Consideration of these issues leads naturally to the next question, that of the possible harmonisation of insurance contract law across the European Union.

The third issue is that of the regulation of the services and activities of insurance intermediaries, whose role in the selling and negotiation of insurance contracts is both crucial and highly problematic.

Finally, the Chapter examines the role of Ombudsman schemes in the UK and elsewhere in the European Union. These schemes have evolved to a point where they play an increasingly important role in dispute resolution within the insurance industry. Indeed, in the UK it is no exaggeration to say that in the context of consumer insurance the decisions of the Ombudsman are of much greater significance than the decisions of the courts.

1. PRIVATE INTERNATIONAL LAW

In the case of any contract with an international element the rules of private international law may become relevant. For present purposes there is an international element in any case where the parties are resident in different States or where they are resident in the same State but the risk is situated in a third State. If the insurance contract becomes the subject of litigation, actual or proposed, it will be necessary to consider the three fundamental questions of private international law.

1. Which court has jurisdiction to try the action?
2. Which system of law applies to the case?
3. Where can any judgment in the action be enforced?

These three questions are at a general level the subject of substantial bodies of case law as well as of certain international conventions. In the particular context of insurance, the Directives also make a number of relevant provisions. A very brief account of the general principles of private international law appears below. Fuller accounts may be found in the major textbooks in this area.[1]

2.   JURISDICTION

It is usually possible to bring proceedings in any place where the defendant has assets or has its principal place of business. However, proceedings may be started in any jurisdiction, and it is then for the courts of that system to decide whether or not to accept the case. A defendant may seek to have an action in one jurisdiction stayed on the ground that this is not the appropriate forum, though it is fair to say that in most systems courts are reluctant to decline jurisdiction if there is any plausible connection between the case and that jurisdiction. Further problems may then arise if there are simultaneous proceedings in more than one jurisdiction, not least because these proceedings could in theory come to different results in relation to the same matter. The situation ought not to be allowed to arise, but can only be prevented if the courts of at least one country involved are prepared to decline jurisdiction.

3.   CHOICE OF LAW

The general private international law rule is that the law applicable to a contract is that chosen by the parties,[2] either expressly or by implication. In the absence of such a choice private international law adopts a doctrine known as the Proper Law of the Contract. This doctrine may be briefly stated as being that the law applicable to a contract in the absence of any choice of law by the parties is the law of that system with which the contract has its closest and most significant connection. Determining which system that is in any given case may be a matter of some difficulty. In the particular context of insurance it is necessary to have in mind the provisions of the Second generation Directives which deal with choice of law in relation to policies sold on a services basis. The provisions, more fully dealt with in Chapter 3, create a presumption that the proper law will normally be that of the policyholder's home State, though this presumption can be rebutted by express provisions. However, these presumptions do not apply in the case of policies sold on an establishment basis under the Third generation Directives.

---

1   The leading text is Dicey and Morris, *The Conflict of Laws*, Sweet & Maxwell; less detailed accounts may be found in Morris, *Conflict of Laws*, Sweet & Maxwell and Cheshire and North, *Principles of Private International Law*, Butterworths.

2   *Vita Food Products Inc. v Unus Shipping Co* [1939] A.C. 277. See also Chapter 3.

In these cases the Proper Law of the Contract doctrine will apply unless there is an express choice of law clause. It is suggested that the inclusion of an express choice of law clause ought to be standard practice in any insurance policy which is capable of being sold across national boundaries (and in the light of the Third Directives provisions that will include virtually all insurance policies currently sold).

4. ENFORCEMENT

Once a judgment has been obtained in a private international law case, the next question is how to enforce it. To the extent that the defendant has assets in the country where the judgment was obtained, this issue is no different from that which arises in trying to enforce a judgment in a purely domestic case. The problem becomes more acute where it is sought to enforce against assets in another country, for in this event it is normally necessary to have the assistance of the legal system of that other country. For the purpose of arranging the giving of such assistance there are a number of international conventions under which countries agree to respect judgments given in each other's courts. Thus, a foreign judgment under which a sum of money is payable may be enforced in England under the Administration of Justice Act 1920 or the Foreign Judgments (Reciprocal Enforcement) Act 1933. In the case of judgments rendered in the courts of Member States of the European Union, the provisions of the Civil Jurisdiction and Judgments Act 1982 are of great assistance in securing enforcement in England.

5. THE HARMONISATION OF INSURANCE CONTRACT LAW

The difficulties discussed above arising from differences in insurance contract law between the legal systems of Member States show that there would be considerable advantages from the point of view of developing the internal market if the insurance contract law of the Member States could be wholly or at least substantially harmonised.

Unfortunately, this project is much easier to state than to implement. Two principal reasons for this may be advanced. The first is that it is neither possible nor sufficient to deal only with matters of insurance contract law. Such an approach is not possible because there is no clear way of delineating the scope of a subject called 'insurance contract law'. The law relating to the contractual aspects of insurance (as distinct from the regulatory or fiscal aspects) is not a discrete subject but a part of the more general contract law of each Member State. Although there are some aspects of insurance contract law which are particular to insurance contracts,[3] many other aspects have the same rules as other types of contracts. Harmonisation of insurance contract law would therefore involve harmonisation of contract law more generally, a much more radical and far–reaching proposal.

Even if (insurance) contract law generally could be harmonised, that would not be sufficient to deal with difficulties caused by differences in legal systems, because disparities in fiscal treatment would remain. Thus, significant areas of tax law would also have to be harmonised. This is, if anything an even more difficult proposition than the harmonisation of contract law, for taxation is commonly regarded by individual Member States as a matter of the most fundamental importance to sovereignty. Certainly, it is noticeable that in the development of the Internal Market very little progress has been made in harmonising direct taxation rules[4] (indirect taxation is of course already harmonised through the system of Value Added Tax). Within the context of the system of direct taxation as a whole the taxation of insurance business is a relatively small part, and it is therefore unlikely that there will be a fundamental realignment of national tax systems simply to accommodate the wish to create the Internal Market in Insurance. It follows that the problems of insurance taxation are only realistically likely to be addressed in the context of a more general harmonisation of direct taxation, a process which is not likely to happen in the foreseeable future.

The second fundamental difficulty goes to the root of the very suggestion that there should or could be harmonisation of legal systems. It must be borne in mind that there are within the European Union two major families of legal systems, the common law family and the civil law family. The former is found only in the United Kingdom and the Republic of Ireland, all the other common law countries being former parts of the British Empire which are not now Member States of the European Union. The remaining thirteen Member States, as well as the countries of the European Economic Area (Norway, Iceland and Liechtenstein) and most of the current applicants for membership, are civil law countries. There remain substantial differences of culture and approach between the two systems. For present purposes it is

---

3   Commonly these includes such matters as the duty of disclosure, the rules as to insurable interest, classification of terms and subrogation.

4   Some limited progress is achieved by Directives 90/434, 90/435 and 90/463, which deal with the repatriation of profits and with the taxation of mergers and divisions. However, the very limited nature of these Directives merely serves to emphasise the extreme difficulty of making progress in these areas, a difficulty which is in turn a function of the very politically sensitive nature of questions relating to taxation and to the possible harmonisation of tax systems.

sufficient to mention two major differences. The first is that civil law systems are codified systems, in which the law is essentially found in the Code, whereas common law systems have traditionally been uncodified systems in which the law is primarily found in the case law (though in many areas of law the common law systems have in the past fifty years seen increasing statutory codification). The second, possibly arising from the first, is that civil law systems are usually seen as being less flexible in their approach than common law systems. To put the same point in another way, common law systems are more unpredictable and even capricious than civil law systems. It is a commonplace of discussions between civil lawyers and common lawyers that the two cultures think about law in significantly different ways, and that these differences go beyond mere differences of detail in individual legal rules. It might with justice be said that a common lawyer and a civil lawyer confronted with a legal problem and the same set of codified rules to deal with it, would nevertheless approach the matters in different ways and might even come to different results.

A.   The Draft Insurance Contract Law Directive

In 1979 there was a proposal from the Commission for a Directive to harmonise insurance contract law.[5] Although the proposal never got beyond the draft stage, it is instructive to consider its contents in order to see which areas of the subject were to be harmonised and what techniques of harmonisation were to be adopted.

As is usual with Directives, the recitals provide some useful background information on the context of the Directive. The recitals provide a reminder that the Second Directives introduced a system for the freedom to provide services, and that choice of law questions were resolved in some cases by opting for the law of the State where the risk is situated and in others by allowing the parties freedom of choice. However, they then also remind the reader that these solutions were adopted 'pending subsequent co–ordination of national rules governing insurance contracts'.

This is followed by the assertion that:

> 'such co–ordination, by establishing a balance between the interests of the insurer on the one hand and the protection of the policyholder and the insured person on the other, is likely to enable freedom of choice to be extended and thus to facilitate the exercise of freedom to provide services'.

---

5   OJ C190/2 28.7.79.

This bold statement of the merits of harmonisation of insurance contract law reads rather oddly in the light of the subsequent history of this area of European law. It is particularly interesting to contrast the assertion in the recitals to the Third Directives to the effect that the harmonisation of insurance contract law is not a precondition to the creation of the Internal Market.[6] Of course the two statements are not strictly incompatible, since one asserts that harmonisation is valuable, whilst the other only declares that it is not essential, but there can be no doubt that the two statements, separated by a distance of thirteen years, reflect two significantly different philosophies of the development of Europe. In 1979 it still seemed possible to aspire to a true Single Market with uniform laws, but by 1992 the political realities looked somewhat different; the Commission therefore took a pragmatic view, preferring to concentrate on developments which would be useful and attainable, even if not ideal.

The recitals also give a clear indication of which areas of insurance law the Commission then regarded as being of fundamental importance. These were the consequences resulting from the conduct of the policyholder at the time of the conclusion of and in the course of the contract concerning the declaration of the risk and of the claim; secondly the policyholder's attitude with regard to the measures to be taken in the event of a claim; thirdly, questions relating to the existence of cover depending on the payment of the premium; fourthly, the duration of the contract; fifthly, the position of insured persons who are not policyholders. The Directive also deals with another matter, namely the provision of information to the policyholder.

In considering the scope of the Directive it should firstly be noted that certain classes of insurance are excluded from its provisions. Life assurance is excluded in its entirety. In the non–life category the excluded classes are railway rolling stock, aircraft, ships, sea, lake and river and canal vessels, goods in transit, aircraft liability, liability for ships, sea, lake and river and canal vessels, credit and suretyship. These classes are defined by reference to the classes of insurance for authorisation purposes listed in the Annex to the First non–Life Directive,[7] an approach which would greatly facilitate the task of deciding whether a particular policy fell within the Directive. The excluded classes are all types of insurance exclusively or predominantly taken out by policyholders acting in the course of a business of theirs (commonly known as commercial lines policies) though of course they by no means exhaust the range of commercial lines policies. The effect of this is that virtually all personal lines policies would fall within the Directive, but that many commercial lines policies would be excluded.

---

6   See Chapter 4.

7   For the details of this Directive see Chapter 3.

The substantive provisions of the Directive proceed by conferring rights and imposing duties on both policyholder and insurer. As is usual in the case of Directives, the provisions are not directly applicable, but art. 13 of the Directive requires the Member States to implement all measures necessary to comply with the Directive within 18 months of its notification, and forthwith to inform the Commission of those measures. In the following discussion of the rights and duties arising from the Directive proposals it should therefore be borne in mind that the Directive describes only the result to be reached – its terms do not directly dictate the drafting of any implementing provisions.

B. Provision of Information to the Policyholder

Art. 2 imposes minimum requirements as to the documentation to be supplied to the policyholder under any contract of insurance covered by the Directive. A document must be issued showing the name and address or head office of the contracting parties, the subject matter of the insurance and a description of the risks covered, the amount insured or the method of calculating it, the dates on which premiums or contributions fall due, the duration of the contract and the times at which cover commences and expires and, where it applies, the time of automatic renewal. Pending the issue of such a document, the policyholder is entitled to receive at the earliest opportunity a document which attests to the existence of an insurance contract and gives at least details of the parties, the subject matter, the risks covered and the amount insured or the method of calculating it. If after the contract has come into force any change occurs which affects the information required to be given, this change must forthwith be notified to the policyholder. If provisional cover is provided, the policyholder is entitled to receive a document certifying that such cover has in fact been provided and showing at least the parties, the subject matter, the risks covered, the amount insured or the method of calculating it, the duration of the contract and the times at which cover commences and expires. Art. 2.5 provides that all the documents so far referred to have only a probative value. This appears to mean that the contents of the documents are not conclusive between the parties as to the terms of the contract, though it is hard to see how an insurer would ever be allowed to claim that the terms of the contract were less favourable to the policyholder than those contained in the documentation provided in fulfilment of the art. 2 requirements. The contract must be drafted in the language of the Member State whose law is applicable, except that the policyholder is entitled to stipulate as a condition precedent to the conclusion of the contract that all documents relating to the contract be translated into the language of his habitual residence, provided such language is an official language of the Community. This provision must be understood in the light of the rules in the

Second non–Life Directive relating to applicable law. These rules, explained in detail in Chapter 3, would usually have the result that the law of the policyholder's habitual residence was the applicable law, so the residual right to demand a translation would not often be of practical significance. It should also be observed that the Directive only gives the policyholder the right to demand this translation as a condition precedent to the conclusion of the contract; moreover, no sanction is provided for failure to comply with the requirement. The practical effect appears to be that an insurer can easily refuse to provide the translation at the probable cost of losing the business.

C. Policyholder's Conduct at Time of Conclusion of Contract

Art. 3 deals with this question. The policyholder must declare to the insurer any circumstances of which he is aware which may influence the insurer's assessment or acceptance of the risk, other than those of which the insurer is already aware or which are common knowledge. Where the insurer has asked specific written questions about a particular circumstance, this is rebuttably presumed to be relevant to the assessment and acceptance of the risk.

It will be observed that this provision does nothing more than state the duty of disclosure in respect of a contract of insurance, a duty recognised in all developed legal systems. It is not entirely clear whether the presumption of relevance for specific questions accurately reproduces English law, though it is fair to say that there is no reported case in English law where a specific question has been held to be immaterial. Certainly the formulation in art. 3 accurately embodies the notion that the duty of disclosure is a positive duty not dependent on the asking of questions.

Subsequent clauses of art. 3 go on to deal with the consequences of a failure to disclose. If circumstances unknown to both parties when the contract was made subsequently come to light or if the policyholder (innocently)[8] fails to comply with the duty of disclosure, the insurer then has two months from the date on which he becomes aware of the fact to propose an amendment to the contract. It is clear from the wording of this provision that the amendment spoken of is not intended to be a straightforward avoidance of the contract, but an appropriate adjustment of its terms to reflect the fact which has now come to light. The policyholder has 15 days from the date on which he receives the proposal for the amendment in which

---

[8] Although art. 3.2 does not use this word, it is clear from arts 3.3 and 3.4, dealing with negligent and fraudulent non–disclosure respectively, that art. 3.2 is intended to apply only in cases of innocent non–disclosure.

to accept or reject it. If he rejects it or fails to reply, the insurer may terminate the contract by giving 15 days' notice. He must thereupon make a proportionate return of premium. If a claim arises before the contract is amended or before termination of the contract has taken effect, the insurer must provide the agreed cover.

It can be seen that these parts of art. 3.2 differ significantly from the English law position on innocent non–disclosure. Where the policyholder has neither actual nor constructive knowledge of the fact in question, there is no duty to disclose, and the policy is fully valid.[9] By contrast, non–disclosure of a fact of which there is constructive knowledge renders the policy voidable in its entirety, with no obligation to offer any amendment. In the case of a personal lines policy this is to some extent mitigated by the Statements of Insurance Practice, issued by the Association of British Insurers. Most major insurers belong to this Association and to the Insurance Ombudsman Bureau,[10] which makes decisions in the light of these Statements. The Statements require insurers to limit disclosure to facts in the actual knowledge of the proposer and which a reasonable proposer could have been expected to disclose. Although the Statements do not have the force of law, the binding character of decisions of the Insurance Ombudsman will lead to the same effect in most cases.

In the case of avoidance, all the premium must be returned. The fact that the claim arises before the right to avoid has been exercised is immaterial – it is common for the non–disclosure not to come to light until the claim is made and investigated. Clearly, the provisions of art. 3.2 represent an attempt to balance the interests of the parties in what is acknowledged as a difficult area,[11] though the solutions which they adopt are somewhat different from those in use in English law. It is to be observed, however, that English law has long been regarded as unduly harsh to policyholders in this respect. Indeed, since the Directive was proposed, the decision of the House of Lords in *Pine Top v Pan Atlantic*[12] has gone some way towards alleviating these difficulties. That decision introduces into the law a concept not recognised in 1979 and certainly absent from the Directive, namely the need for a proven causal link between the non–disclosure and the entering into the policy.

An unresolved issue in the draft Directive concerns the nature of the amendment to be proposed. The spirit of the Directive would seem to suggest that the idea of the amendment is simply that the contract should be

---

9   *Joel v Law Union and Crown Insurance Co* [1908] 2 K.B. 863 C.A.
10 See below.
11 McGee, A., *Utmost Good Faith in the Third Millennium*, in Feldman and Meisel (eds), Corporate and Commercial Law: Modern Developments, (1996) LLP.
12 [1994] 3 All E.R. 581 H.L.

brought into line with what would have happened if the fact had been disclosed, but the wording of art. 3 does not compel the conclusion that the insurer is forbidden to propose a more extensive amendment. Indeed, the wording would seem to allow the insurer, if confronted with a minor non-disclosure, to propose an amendment so major that no reasonable policyholder would be likely to agree to it. In effect, this means that the insurer can always avoid for non-disclosure, since the result of such a proposal will presumably be a rejection by the policyholder, whereupon the right to avoid will arise.

Art. 3.3 then deals with the case where the policyholder has failed to disclose and 'may be considered to have acted improperly'. As suggested above, this rather vague expression appears to relate to cases of negligent (but not fraudulent) non-disclosure. There are two important differences between the consequences of innocent non-disclosure and those of negligent non-disclosure. In the case of negligent non-disclosure the insurer always has the option to terminate the contract, ie he is not obliged to propose an amendment, though he may do so if he chooses. If an amendment is proposed, the consequences are the same as in the case of innocent non-disclosure. If the contract is terminated, there is a proportionate return of premium. The second major difference occurs if a claim arises before amendment or termination. In the case of innocent non-disclosure such a claim must be met in full, but in the case of negligent non-disclosure the doctrine of proportionality applies, the insurer's liability being limited to the proportion of the claim represented by the ratio between the premium actually paid and the premium which would have been paid if the policyholder had declared the risk correctly. This principle has also been applied in the United Kingdom by the Insurance Ombudsman. Its attractions are obvious – it keeps the policy alive, thus providing some cover, and at the same time limits that cover to what would have been obtainable for the premium on the basis of full disclosure. It appears to work well in civil law countries, where the terms of policies normally require approval in advance and the only possible responses to disclosure of facts are premium loadings or the outright rejection of the proposal. Its introduction into English law as a matter of entitlement rather than subject to the discretion of the Insurance Ombudsman might be more problematic because there are more possible responses to the disclosure of information. These include limiting the scope of the cover, imposing conditions precedent to recovery (such as security conditions in household policies) or limiting the sum assured. The doctrine of proportionality does not cope well with these variations.

Art. 3.4 deals with fraudulent non-disclosure (where the policyholder has failed to disclose 'with the intention of deceiving the insurer'). Here, as might be expected, the consequences are far more draconian. The insurer may terminate the contract within two months of becoming aware of the fraud. There is no liability in respect of any claim; moreover, the insurer may retain all premiums paid and is entitled to claim all outstanding premiums, though it may be doubted whether this last clause will often be invoked in practice.

In the case of both negligent and fraudulent non–disclosure the insurer may recover sums paid out to the insurer under a mistake as to legal liability, ie where the insurer pays a claim, not having discovered the non–disclosure. On the later discovery of the non–disclosure the claim may be adjusted, the insurer recovering a proportion in the case of negligent non–disclosure, the whole claim in the case of fraud.[13]

As might be expected, the insurer bears the burden of proving negligence or fraud.[14]

These provisions, taken together, represent a very sensible and rational approach to the issues of non–disclosure, although they fall some way short of being an exhaustive account of the subject. Their adoption into domestic law could only improve that law.

D.   Policyholder's Conduct During Contract

Art. 4 deals with problems arising from increase of risk. In English law there is no general principle that alterations of risk after the contract has been entered into have to be disclosed to the insurer. All the reported cases[15] deal with policies which had express increase of risk clauses, and in all of them the insurer's attempt to rely on the clause failed. Art. 4.1 requires the policyholder to declare to the insurer any new circumstances or change of circumstance *of which the insurer has requested notification in the contract.*[16] There is no suggestion of a more general duty to notify increase of risk. The declaration is to be made not later than the time when the risk increases where this is attributable to an intentional act of the policyholder. In all other cases it must be made immediately the policyholder becomes aware of the increase.

The insurer has two months from the date of the notification to propose

---

[13]   Art. 5.

[14]   Art. 3.5.

[15]   *Shaw v Robberds,* (1837), 6 Ad & El 75, *Beauchamp v National Mutual,* [1937], 3 All E.R. 19, *Exchange Thatre Ltd v Iron Trades Mutual* [1984], 1 Lloyd's Reports 149, *Hadenfayre v British National Insurance Society Ltd* [1984], 2 Lloyd's Reports 393.

[16]   Emphasis added.

an amendment. The procedure in relation to such proposed amendments is the same as that in art. 3.2 for amendments arising from cases of innocent non–disclosure.

A failure to give the appropriate notice does not give rise to any sanction if the new or changed circumstance is not likely to appreciably and permanently increase the risk and lead to an increase in premium. In practical terms this means that the general obligation to notify, even when contained in the policy, must be understood as being subject to a threshold for substantial changes. Minor changes and temporary changes (apparently even major but temporary changes) do not require to be disclosed. However, where the change was one which should have been notified and was not notified, the insurer again has two months from the date of discovering the failure to notify in which to propose an amendment under the art. 3.2 procedure (or the art. 3.3 procedure in the case of a negligent failure to notify). In the case of a fraudulent failure to notify an increase of risk, the insurer may terminate the policy within two months of becoming aware of the circumstances, but may keep all the premiums paid and is entitled to all outstanding premiums. He is not liable for any claim arising after the increase in the risk, even if the loss was not attributable to the increase of risk. As with art. 3, payments made by the insurer which he was by reason of art. 4 not bound to make are recoverable.

Art. 6 deals with reductions in the risk. If during the policy the risk diminishes appreciably and permanently because of circumstances other than those covered in the contract, and if this justifies a reduction in the premium, the policyholder shall be entitled to terminate the contract without compensation if the insurer does not agree to reduce the premium proportionately. This provision gives rise to some considerable difficulties of interpretation. Firstly, the question whether the risk has diminished 'appreciably' is obviously one of degree. The requirement that the diminution must be permanent will no doubt serve to reduce substantially the range of cases to which art. 6 applies. However, the most difficult part of art. 6.1 is the reference to the diminution 'justifying' a reduction in premium. The article gives no further explanation of when a permanent and appreciable diminution in the risk would justify a reduction in premium. Since this requirement is additional to that of the diminution of risk, it is to be assumed that not all permanent and appreciable reductions would justify a reduction in the premium. This is unfortunate, since a natural way to interpret the reference to justification would be to ask whether the reduced risk, if it had existed at inception, would have led to a reduced premium. The problem with this approach is that in almost every case a risk which was permanently and appreciably less than the one actually declared would almost always have justified a reduced premium. Perhaps this approach is still available, however. Given that the requirement for permanent diminution will remove many cases from the scope of art. 6 anyway, it might be thought that most other cases would justify a reduction in premium, so that the reference to this adds little to the test. If the insurer refuses the policyholder's request for a reduction in premium, or if he fails to reply to the request within 15 days, the policyholder may terminate the contract and claim a proportionate return of premium. The mechanics of this system also call for examination. First, the right to terminate arises only if a reduction of premium is justified and the insurer does not agree to a *proportionate* reduction of premium. The insurer is not obliged to accept a request for a disproportionate reduction of premium. It is easy to see that there might be ample room for dispute over the policyholder's expectations as to the reduction in premium. However, much of this difficulty might in practice be eliminated by the policyholder's need to make a simple calculation. Even if the insurer refuses the request for a reduction in premium, it will not be worthwhile for the policyholder to attempt to terminate the contract and obtain a refund of premium unless he can in fact get cover elsewhere for the remaining period of the policy more cheaply than his current insurer is prepared to offer.

The provisions for reduction of premium have no counterpart in English law, where there is no right to a reduction of premium during the term of the policy, even in the event of substantial reduction of the risk.

E.   Policyholder's Attitude to Measures to be Taken in the Event of a Claim

Art. 8 deals with this subject. If a claim arises, the policyholder must take all reasonable steps to avoid or reduce the consequences. In particular, instructions from the insurer or compliance with specific provisions on this point contained in the contract shall be considered reasonable. This provision appears poorly drafted. The statement that instructions from the insurer are deemed reasonable must mean only that they are deemed reasonable for the purposes of this clause, so that an insured who complies with them can always claim to have acted reasonably for these purposes. It cannot mean that failure to comply with such instructions is always deemed unreasonable, since there could obviously be cases where the instructions given by the insurer were in fact unreasonable and even impracticable. In such a case it cannot be right to say that the policyholder is bound to comply with the instructions on pain of having his claim reduced in whole or in part. The costs incurred by the policyholder in mitigating his loss, carrying out the insurer's instructions or taking any steps required by the policy are borne by the insurer.[17]

The general requirement to mitigate loss is in accordance with the principles of English law, and it is common to find an express clause to this effect in policies in the UK. There is no English authority to suggest that the insurer's instructions must always be complied with.

A failure to mitigate as required by art. 8.1 gives the insurer a right to claim damages for the loss which he thereby suffers. In effect this means that any additional loss caused by the failure to mitigate (any loss which would have been avoided by proper mitigation) falls on the policyholder rather than on the insurer. This again corresponds to the general English law principle in relation to mitigation of loss. Art. 8.5 goes further by providing that a failure to mitigate which is intended to cause the insurer loss or to deceive him releases the insurer from all liability to make payment in respect of the claim, even for that part of the loss which is genuine and cannot reasonably be mitigated. This situation is likely to be rare, but the treatment proposed by the Directive is arguably more lenient than that afforded by English law, where deliberate failure to mitigate might well be regarded as a breach of the ongoing duty of utmost good faith which would give the insurer the right to terminate the policy as well as refusing to pay out on the particular claim.

Art. 9 contains more general provisions dealing with the claims process. The policyholder is required to declare any claim to the insurer in accordance with the conditions and time limits laid down in the policy. Any time limits imposed must be reasonable, and national laws are allowed to fix time limits for certain classes of insurance. So far as English law is concerned, the Statements of Practice forbid the fixing of strict time limits in personal lines policies; instead the obligation should only be notification within a reasonable time. This rule does not contravene the Directive. The insurer may also require the policyholder to produce all the necessary information and documents on the circumstances and consequences of the claim. Negligent failure to comply with the requirements of art. 9 gives the insurer a right to damages, though this will only be relevant where the insurer can show that he has suffered loss as a result of the non–compliance. It seems that this will rarely arise, since the most common response of an insurer to failure to comply with a time limit or failure to supply the necessary documentation will be to reject the claim in whole or in part. Art. 9.4 follows the general pattern of the Directive by releasing the insurer from all liability in respect of the claim if the failure to comply is shown to have been done with the intention of causing the insurer loss or deceiving him.

---

[17]   Art. 8.2.

F. Existence of Cover Depending on Payment of Premium

Art. 7 deals with payment of premium. Failure to pay the premium in whole, or in part may be penalised only after a period of grace of at least 15 days, the time to run from the date on which the policyholder is notified, in writing and after the payment is due, of the penalty. The practical effect of this is that the period of grace will always be somewhat more than 15 days from the date on which the premium was originally due.

G. Duration of Contract

Art. 10 contains provisions dealing with rights to terminate the contract. The Directive allows termination without notice only where one of the parties has failed to perform his obligations with the intention of deceiving the other party, This general principle reflects the specific provisions in the Directive on disclosure, increase of risk and claims process, but it also goes beyond that, for it would require Member States to change their laws to remove any more general right for either party to cancel without notice.

In the absence of any breach of obligation, the general rule is that termination is allowed only upon notice of at least 15 days, the time running from the date on which notice is given. If the policy contains a provision for automatic renewal, this renewal is for a period of not more than one year (the exact period depending on the policy and/or the national law) unless either party gives notice of termination at least two months before the expiry of the current insurance period. If the policy is for a period of more than three years, the policyholder may terminate it at the end of the third year or of any subsequent year by giving at least two months' notice. This right (which is not conferred on insurers) is additional to the right described in the previous sentence. Finally, art. 10 allows the Member States to restrict further the insurer's right to cancel long–term contracts (which in this context can only be a reference to permanent health insurance contracts, since life assurance itself is excluded from the scope of the Directive).

H. Position of Insured Persons who are not Policyholders

Art. 11 deals with the situation where the person insured is not the policyholder. Given that the Directive does not apply to life assurance at all, it appears that this will be a relatively rare situation in English law, since the doctrine of insurable interest normally makes it very difficult for one person with no personal interest in the policy to insure on behalf of another. What is possible in English law is for one person with an insurable interest to insure on behalf of himself and another person who also has an insurable interest. In this event there could be a person who was insured but not the policyholder. A possible modern example in English law would be a group health insurance scheme for the employees of a particular company. It is usual to issue the policy to the company, but it is arguable that it is the individual employees who are insured.[18] The scheme of art. 10 is that, so far as possible, an insured person who is not a policyholder should be treated in the same way as a policyholder. Thus, he benefits from the right to have the insurer pay his costs incurred in mitigating his losses in accordance with art. 8. On the other hand he is also under the same obligations as the policyholder in relation to disclosure, change of risk and notifying claims to the extent that he has knowledge of the contract and is able to comply with these obligations.

I.   Parties' Contractual Freedom

Art. 12 allows the parties to agree on terms other than those provided for in the Directive, provided that these are more favourable to the policyholder, injured person or insured third party, than those contained in the Directive. Thus, the protections which the Directive gives to policyholders are a minimum standard rather than a maximum limit. On the other hand the Member States are not allowed to derogate from the provisions of the Directives except where the Directive itself specifically authorises this.

J.   Conclusion

The Draft Directive never made progress beyond being a draft, and at the present day it rarely merits more than a brief mention in any history of European Insurance Law. In one sense this may be considered justified, since there is now obviously no prospect that it will ever become law, nor does it seem likely that there will be any serious attempt to harmonise insurance contract law. On the other hand some interesting points may be extracted from the Directive. First, it is clear that any harmonisation process would have to start from the position of respecting the existing well–established insurance law of the individual Member States. It might be helpful to draw an analogy with the very extensive harmonisation programme in company law, another area which had well–developed national rules, but which it has

---

[18]   This is the view taken by the Insurance Ombudsman, for whom the question is one of jurisdiction.

proved possible to harmonise. The Draft Insurance Law Directive might be regarded as laying down some basic principles upon which later Directives could build, each Directive perhaps dealing with a limited range of contentious areas, with the Directives collectively building into a coherent set of principles for the subject. Second, the existing draft should readily convince an English insurance lawyer of the merits of a scheme of this kind. A number of points have already been identified on which English law is either unclear or simply deficient. These gaps could be remedied in a suitable set of Directives.[19] Third, in a number of areas the approaches proposed are more favourable to the policyholder than English law has traditionally been. Few people could seriously doubt that English insurance law has long been sadly deficient in this respect, and the approach of the Directive, even as long ago as 1979, offers at least a sensible way forward. Fourth, the range of the Directive is limited, and the proposals it contains are noticeably modest and reasonable. It is hard to see why the enactment and implementation of this Directive should be seen as a threat to the interests or sovereignty of any of the Member States.

K.   The Unfair Terms in Consumer Contracts Directive[20]

This Directive required Member States to introduce into their law provisions striking down unfair terms in consumer contracts generally. The following discussion must therefore be understood in the light of the fact that the regulations apply to all types of consumer contract.

The scheme of the Directive is essentially[21] that terms in consumer contracts may be invalidated if, contrary to the requirement of good faith, they create a significant imbalance between the parties, to the detriment of the consumer.[22] However, terms are not subject to this test if they are 'core terms' and are expressed in plain, intelligible language.[23]

It is provided that:

---

19   Though it is of course true that this argument can be seen as no more than a general argument in favour of codification, which need not come from a Directive.

20   J. Davey, Unfair Terms In Consumer Insurance Contracts, paper delivered at 1997 *Insurance and the Law Conference*, Leeds University, 10 April 1997.

21   For a fuller account see Adams and Brownsword, *'Key Issues in Contract Law'*, (Butterworths, 1995), Chapter 8; Duffy [1993], J.B.L. 67; Dean (1993), 56 M.L.R. 581; Collins (1994), 14 O.J.L.S. 229; Brownsword & Howells [1995], J.B.L. 243 and MacDonald [1994], J.B.L. 243.

22   Reg. 4(1).

23   Reg. 6.

'In so far as it is in plain, intelligible language, no assessment shall be made of the fairness of any term which –

(a)   defines the main subject matter of the contract, or

(b)   concerns the adequacy of the price or remuneration, as against the goods or services sold or supplied.'[24]

However, Recital 19 to the Directive declares that the logic of the Directive requires that in insurance contracts terms which define the risk or the insurer's liability be exempted from control. The existing literature in this field shows that the application of this principle is far from clear. Firstly, it is uncertain what status the Recital has in the face of the apparently clear words of the articles of the Directive. Second, it is unclear what is meant by defining the risk or the insurer's liability. There is, for example, dispute over whether warranties, especially promissory warranties, are clauses which define the risk. There is an exception in respect of any term that has been individually negotiated. A term is not individually negotiated where it is drafted in advance, and where the consumer has been unable to influence the substance of the term.[25]

The enforcement of the Regulations[26] in the UK is in the hands of the Director General of Fair Trading,[27] who has so far taken a strongly consumerist approach to interpretation of the Regulations. In bulletins issued by the Director General,[28] there are a number of statements that could be seen as supporting a wide view of this provision. In particular, it is mentioned that the use of legal terms of art is contrary to this requirement. Thus terms such as *'force majeure'*, and 'consequential loss' are used as examples of clauses that are not regarded as being in plain and intelligible language.[29] The Director General expressly states that contract terms must normally be 'within the understanding of ordinary consumers *without legal advice'*.[30] The view of the Director General of Fair Trading does give an indication of circumstances when enforcement will be pursued. However there are as yet no formal decisions, whether by the OFT or by the courts, to resolve any of the problems of interpretation.

---

24   Reg. 3(2).

25   Reg. 3(3).

26   S.I. 1994/3159.

27   Reg. 8.

28   Extensive summaries are available at http://www.open.gov.uk/oft/ofthome.htm.

29   *Unfair Contract Terms – Issue No. 2,* Office of Fair Trading (September, 1996), p. 10.

30   OFT Bulletin No. 2, *op. cit.,* p. 10.

6. INTERMEDIARIES

The role of intermediaries in the creation of insurance contracts is fundamental. It is still the case that the majority of insurance contracts are formed with the aid of at least one intermediary, though it must be admitted that the growth in recent years of direct provision of insurance services by telephone has begun to undermine the traditional role of the intermediary. There are two types of intermediary in an insurance context, the insurance agent and the broker. The former works for the insurer and is employed to sell policies on behalf of the insurer, whereas the latter acts as agent for the policyholder, to whom he owes his duties. The problems arising from the activities of intermediaries are numerous,[31] but for present purposes they may be simply summarised. Insurance agents are mostly paid by commission and may therefore be tempted to sell policies to persons for whom they are not really suitable. This problem, which is especially prevalent in relation to investment policies, is exacerbated by the complexities of most policies; it is often easy for unscrupulous agents to sell policies by misrepresenting their contents. In the case of brokers the problems are perhaps less acute, but it is clear than many brokers operate essentially on the basis of high volumes of relatively low–paying business. In these circumstances it is not surprising that the quality of the advice which they give to policyholders is at best variable.

In the specific context of the Single European Market an additional layer of difficulty is created by the fact that there are significant differences in regulatory structure between Member States, whereas very little has been done towards harmonising the different regulatory systems. In 1976 there was a Directive on Insurance Intermediaries, which was intended as an interim measure pending fuller harmonisation.[32] This Directive did not require Member States to introduce additional regulatory systems for insurance intermediaries. Instead, it sought to deal with the problems of intermediaries who wished to take up business in another Member State, but who found themselves prevented from so doing by existing national rules requiring intermediaries to have particular qualifications. Its approach may be regarded as an early example of the use of techniques of mutual recognition. To this end the Directive sets out levels of experience in an intermediary's home State, which, if satisfactorily proved, must be accepted by a host State as satisfying any national rules as to qualifications for intermediaries. The scheme is of course without practical significance in

---

[31] For a fuller account of the role of intermediaries in insurance law see McGee, *The Law and Practice of Life Assurance Contracts* (Sweet & Maxwell, 1995).

[32] Ellis, p. 147.

those Member States which do not impose qualification requirements for intermediaries at all. Essentially these rules operate by recognising experience in a broker's office in a managerial capacity as satisfying any requirements of practical experience leading to qualification to operate as a broker in another Member State. They do not, however, impose any requirements of formal training. The practical training is to be accepted by itself as sufficient evidence of knowledge and ability. The deficiencies of this scheme are very obvious. Practical experience in a broker's office is no doubt an important part of acquiring the competence to do the job, but it might be thought, for example, that an insurance broker needed at least a rudimentary grasp of the relevant legal rules in the jurisdiction in which he proposes to take up business. However, it would not have been practicable for the Commission to impose a requirement of such legal knowledge on those coming from other jurisdictions, given that many Member States do not impose it on their own nationals. On the other hand, any Member State which does impose this requirement on its own nationals is not allowed to impose the same requirement on those coming from other jurisdictions. This is of course an example of the difficulties arising from differences in legal systems, and the solution adopted may perhaps also be understood in this light. It is instructive to compare the approach adopted some years later in the Mutual Recognition Directive when dealing with freedom to provide legal services. There too the test for competence was set at a low level, apparently in order to encourage and facilitate cross-border services. In both cases it might be argued that market forces will rapidly operate to eliminate the incompetent, though in both cases it is also true that considerable damage might be done to consumers before those market forces took effect.[33]

Although the 1976 Directive is the only Directive in this area, the question of regulation of insurance intermediaries was considered again by the Commission as part of the 1992 Single Market programme. In 1991 a Recommendation on Insurance Intermediaries was issued.[34] Although Recommendations are by their nature not binding on Member States, this document is worthy of attention in the present context. The Recitals to the Recommendation mention the importance of insurance intermediaries in providing a good service to policyholders, the growing importance of competence in these areas as cross-border trade grows and the absence in many Member States of basic rules as to knowledge and ability. They then assert the need for registration of insurance intermediaries and declare that a non-binding Recommendation is likely to be an effective way of achieving

---

[33]　The potential damage to consumers is after all the main justification for regulating the provision of such services in the first place.

[34]　92/48/EEC, 18 December 1992, O.J. 28.1.92.

this objective. As is usual with such Recitals, they offer no rational argument in support of any of these propositions.

There then follow the two substantive provisions of the Recommendation. The first calls on Member States to introduce registration requirements, whilst the second is that they should inform the Commission of the steps they take in this field. The detailed recommendations as to registration requirements are contained in the Appendix to the Recommendation. These would require intermediaries to have appropriate knowledge and expertise, to be persons of good repute and to hold suitable professional liability insurance. Member States would also be allowed to impose capital adequacy requirements. In addition there would be limited ongoing monitoring in the form of annual reporting requirements of the spread of business with different insurance undertakings. It would be a criminal offence to practice as an intermediary without the necessary registration, and the fact of registration would have to be disclosed to the public.

The style of regulation proposed in this Recommendation is readily recognisable by comparison with that applying elsewhere in the financial services sector, involving requirements of competence, coupled with ongoing monitoring (albeit on a limited scale) and possible capital adequacy requirements. The terms of the Recommendation are, as might be expected, more vague than those usual in a Directive, since the intention is to provide guidance and advice rather than to bind Member States as to the result to be achieved. As yet the United Kingdom has not introduced registration requirements along the lines proposed. In the area of life and investment policies there was already fairly stringent regulation in the Financial Services Act 1986 for both tied agents and independent financial advisers. Indeed, this regulation probably goes beyond what is contemplated in the Recommendation. On the other hand there is no registration requirement in general insurance, since the Insurance Brokers Registration Act 1977 creates only a purely voluntary scheme. It remains to be seen whether the EU will in due course be prepared to move from a Recommendation to a Directive, but it is submitted that such a development would be both logical and desirable: logical because the Recitals to the Recommendation assume that a Recommendation is an effective way forward in this area. If that assumption is falsified by experience, then an alternative approach will have to be found; desirable because the Recitals rightly point to the importance of proper standards of competence in this area as well as to the importance of a degree of harmonisation in facilitating the development of a Single Market.

7. THE ROLE OF OMBUDSMAN SCHEMES IN THE EUROPEAN UNION

An important practical area of insurance law and practice relates to customer complaints and the resolution of disputes. This is primarily of importance in cases involving private customers, ie those who do not enter into the policy as part of any business of theirs. It is a notable fact that in many of the Member States arrangements are now in place which allow for the resolution of disputes arising from such policies otherwise than through the ordinary courts of law and, in some instances, according to principles other than those of strict law. It is appropriate here to consider why this situation has come about, to describe the arrangements prevailing in a number of the Member States and to consider the implications of these arrangements for the development of the Internal Market.

A. The Origins of Ombudsman Schemes

Ombudsman schemes originated in the public sector rather than in the private sector,[35] and appear to have made their first appearance in Scandinavia, where they were used as a means of giving redress against oppressive or incompetent action on the part of government. In the United Kingdom the first such scheme was the Parliamentary Commissioner for Administration, created under the Parliamentary Commissioner Act 1967. The Commissioner, commonly referred to as the Ombudsman, investigates allegations of maladministration involving government departments and can make non-binding recommendations for the payment of compensation to citizens who have suffered loss through maladministration. In the public sector there are also Local Government Ombudsmen, properly called Commissioners for Local Administration, who exercise similar functions in relation to local authorities.

It is important to understand why Ombudsman schemes have come to be popular, given that all the societies in which they are found clearly operate on the basis of the rule of law and have highly developed legal systems which are, at least in theory, capable of redressing infringements of legal rights. Three particular issues may be identified. First, developed legal systems tend to be slow in resolving even relatively straightforward matters. Second, such systems also tend to be expensive. Third, the legal rights of citizens against

---

35 The first such scheme in the UK was the Parliamentary Commissioner for Maladministration, popularly known as the Ombudsman, created by the Parliamentary Commissioner Act 1967.

government and of the consumers of financial services are often either unclear or inadequate, the law not having developed at the same pace as the expectations of citizens and consumers. It was felt that a quicker, cheaper, more informal system of resolution, based on legitimate expectations as much as on strict legal rights, was a more appropriate way forward. This was especially the case in relation to financial services, an area of notorious complexity, in which standards of customer service had often been seen to fall far short of modern expectations.

In the private sector most Ombudsman schemes have been in financial services – Insurance, Banking, Building Societies, Investment Management, Pensions, though in more recent years the concept has been extended to Legal Services[36] and, more questionably to Corporate Estate Agents. The proliferation of Ombudsman schemes has also led to the creation of the British and Irish Ombudsman Association, whose members include all the major Ombudsman schemes, and which aims to improve and develop notions of best practice for Ombudsman schemes, as well as acting as a discussion forum for issues of common concern within such schemes.

Although the detailed rules of Ombudsman schemes vary considerably, it is clear that, at least in the private sector, there are a number of structural questions which any scheme must answer. These are:

Is membership of the scheme to be compulsory or optional for those businesses operating in the relevant sector?
The earliest private sector schemes – Insurance and Banking – have adopted a principle of voluntary membership, but later schemes have tended to move away from this approach – all Building Societies are required to belong to an approved Ombudsman scheme,[37] and there is only one approved scheme, whilst the Pensions Ombudsman scheme is created by statute with compulsory membership, and all members of the Personal Investment Authority are required to be members of the PIA Ombudsman Bureau.

According to what principles are decisions to be made?
The modern trend in this area appears to be for schemes to operate more or less according to legal rules. The Insurance Ombudsman scheme is now somewhat out of line in allowing a broader discretion to make a fair and reasonable decision even where this does not accord with legal rules. This trend marks a noticeable move away from the origins of Ombudsman schemes, which were originally conceived as a way of mitigating the

---

[36] Courts and Legal Services Act 1990.
[37] Building Societies Act 1986 s. 81.

harshness of the law, which was regarded as giving consumers too few rights.

Are the decisions of the Ombudsman to be binding on both sides, on only one side (usually the scheme member) or on neither side?
Most schemes adopt a solution in which the decision of the Ombudsman is binding on the member but not on the complaining customer, though exceptionally, decisions of the Pensions Ombudsman are binding on both sides subject only to a right of appeal to the High Court.

B. The Ombudsman Schemes Currently in Operation

The United Kingdom has perhaps the most highly developed and diverse system of Ombudsman schemes to be found anywhere in Europe in the financial services sector.[38] So far as insurance is concerned there are currently two schemes.

The Insurance Ombudsman Bureau is the oldest of the United Kingdom's financial service Ombudsman schemes, dating from 1981. In its original form it dealt with cases of life assurance and insurance–based investment products, as well as with general (ie non–life) cases. The scheme applies only to policyholders insured in their private capacities. Membership on the part of companies is voluntary, though the great majority of the large players[39] in the industry (and most of the small ones) have been members. As the Bureau is a collaboration among product providers, insurance brokers cannot be members and the Ombudsman has no jurisdiction over the activities of brokers. Complaints may be brought by actual or prospective policyholders within six months of reaching deadlock with the company on an issue. Most disputes arising out of policies are covered, though actuarial calculations and matters of underwriting judgment are excluded. Decisions of the Ombudsman are binding on the insurance company but not on the policyholder, who may reject an unfavourable decision and retain the right to take the case through the ordinary courts. The contractual nature of the scheme means that there is no effective means of enforcement – the policyholder cannot enforce a decision of the Ombudsman in court, not being party to the Bureau, whilst the Ombudsman's only remedy for non–compliance is to report the matter to the Council of the Bureau, which exists to safeguard the independence of the Ombudsman. The Council's powers

---

38 McGee, *The Financial Services Ombudsman*, Fourmat 1992.
39 The Co–operative Insurance Society, Dominion Insurance and Liverpool Victoria are the conspicuous exceptions.

then rest largely on persuasion, though the ultimate sanction is to expel a company from membership of the Bureau. Fortunately, in the fifteen years the scheme has been running, there has been no case of a company refusing to honour an award against it.

Without doubt the most important single aspect of the rules of the Insurance Ombudsman scheme is the clause in the Ombudsman's Terms of Reference which require him in every case to make a decision which is 'fair and reasonable' in the circumstances. The effect of this clause is to allow, indeed to oblige, the Ombudsman to depart from the strict rules of insurance law when this is necessary in order to produce a fair solution. It may be observed that the implication of including such a clause in the Terms of Reference is to admit that there will be cases where adherence to the letter of the law will not produce a fair and reasonable result. As was explained in the previous paragraph, a belief in this proposition was one of the factors motivating the original creation of the Bureau.

The importance in practice of a clause such as this inevitably depends heavily on the character of the person holding the office of Ombudsman. It is fair to say that the first holder of the office, James Haswell (1981–88), was relatively unadventurous in developing notions of fair and reasonable behaviour on the part of insurers. This characteristic was more than offset by his successor Julian Farrand (1989–94) who made considerable strides in forcing the industry to confront some of its more arcane and old–fashioned attitudes, though at the price of incurring considerable unpopularity among insurers. The third Insurance Ombudsman, Laurie Slade (1994–96, having been Deputy Ombudsman 1989–94) has proved to be of a less dynamic disposition, but has maintained and built on the reforms initiated by Julian Farrand. He has recently resigned, to be replaced by Walter Merricks, who has at the time of writing no track record which can sensibly be discussed.

The Insurance Ombudsman Bureau has been a considerable success when judged against its original objectives of improving public confidence in the industry and fending off statutory reform of the principles of insurance law. Over the years it has received a steadily rising number of complaints.[40] It is even possible to wonder whether the changed attitudes towards consumers which it has sought to promote could have played some role in the decision of the house of Lords in *Pine Top v Pan Atlantic*,[41] where the

---

[40]   1990=3500, 1991=4500, 1992=6000, 1993=8000 (Source IOB Reports for the various years). Since then there has been something of a decline, following on from the creation in 1994 of the PIA Ombudsman Bureau and the transfer to it of the IOB's functions in relation to financial services cases. In April 1997 the Insurance Ombudsman told the author that cases currently run at about 3000 annually.

[41]   [1994] 3 All E.R. 581.

traditionally harsh law of non–disclosure was somewhat modified in favour of policyholders.

Despite the success of the Bureau, especially in the period from 1989, the deficiencies of the regulatory regime created by the Financial Services Act 1986 (of which the Bureau was not part) became increasingly apparent. In the present context two items in particular are relevant. First, the separation for regulatory purposes of tied agents of insurers from independent brokers[42] was seen to be unsustainable, not least because the numbers of brokers declined while the number of compensation claims against them increased. Second, the absence of a one–stop Ombudsman and regulatory solution for personal investors came to be seen as a serious reproach to the industry. The original Financial Services Act scheme had provided separate regulators for insurance, for investment managers[43] and for Stock Exchange investment.[44] The result of the growing dissatisfaction with this state of affairs was the creation in 1994 of the Personal Investment Authority, which took over the regulatory functions of all these bodies in so far as they related to private investors. As part of this process it became necessary to consider the arrangements for complaints handling in those areas which the PIA was to regulate. It was always clear that having one single regulator in this area would lead to having one single Ombudsman scheme; the question was what form that scheme should take and where it should be located. One possibility was to allocate the task to the Insurance Ombudsman Bureau, which already handled cases against product providers involving insurance–based investment products (by far the largest category of such cases). Despite the apparent logic of this approach the report on complaints handling arrangements commissioned by the PIA and produced by Lord Ackner, recommended a new independent Ombudsman scheme. Two important factors in this decision were the voluntary character of IOB membership, whereas membership of the new scheme was to be compulsory, and the very broad discretion exercised by the Insurance Ombudsman under cover of the fair and reasonable clause, a provision which was not to be inserted in the Terms of Reference of the new scheme. It was therefore decided to create a new organisation, called the Personal Investment Authority Ombudsman Bureau, to handle complaints against PIA members. Membership of PIA is compulsory for all product providers and independent intermediaries dealing in personal investment products, a term which includes investment insurance policies, Personal Equity Plans, unit trusts and equity investments aimed at non–commercial purchasers, but does not

---

42　The former being regulated by LAUTRO, the latter by FIMBRA.

43　IMRO.

44　The SFA.

include deposit accounts, wherever held. All members of PIA are required to be members of the PIA Ombudsman Bureau.

PIAOB is a very different creature from the IOB. The absence of a fair and reasonable clause from its Terms of Reference makes it in effect a version of a judicial trial of the case, the differences between PIAOB and a judicial trial being that PIAOB does not normally have oral hearings[45] and a decision by the Ombudsman in favour of the company does not bind the policyholder (though the company must honour a decision against it unless it chooses to take the matter to court). As in the case of the IOB, the effectiveness of PIAOB has depended very heavily on the character of the Ombudsman. Stephen Edell was appointed to be the first PIA Ombudsman in 1994, having previously been Building Societies Ombudsman since 1987. In order to assess his performance in the role it is necessary to be aware of the context of his appointment and of the creation of PIA. The idea of merging LAUTRO and FIMBRA proved extremely controversial, with some major financial services players holding out for a long time before agreeing to join;[46] there was thus in 1994 some serious doubt whether PIA would ever get off the ground. In these circumstances it was clearly crucial to appoint as the first PIA Ombudsman someone who could command the confidence of the industry; Stephen Edell amply met this criterion, having established a track record as a good lawyer[47] with sound judgment, a vital attribute since the jurisdiction of the PIA Ombudsman is based essentially on deciding cases in accordance with the law, who was prepared to proceed cautiously in developing the principles on which an Ombudsman should operate, this attribute being vital in order to reassure the industry. The first two years of the operation of the scheme[48] have confirmed that the scheme is less radical than the IOB scheme and that Stephen Edell's cautious, meticulous approach has largely succeeded in reassuring the industry. Stephen Edell retired in June 1997, and was succeeded by Tony Holland, a former President of the Law Society. He will need to tread skilfully the path between strict adherence to the law and the development of better standards of conduct within the industry.

---

[45] Though these are possible and are used in a very small number of cases.

[46] The alternative was to opt for direct regulation by the Securities and Investments Board. The largest UK insurer, the Prudential, took that course in 1994 and is to this day not a member of PIA, though it now seems likely that this situation will be remedied before the end of 1997.

[47] He had been a Law Commissioner earlier in his career, after holding partnerships in two London solicitors firms.

[48] See the Annual Reports for 1994–5 and 1995–6.

It is tempting to conclude this section on Ombudsman schemes in the United Kingdom by saying that the position is in a state of flux, so that no proper conclusions can be drawn. The truth is that, for one reason or another, the position has been in a state of flux for some years past, and is likely to continue in that state for some time to come. The task of drawing conclusions cannot be shirked on this ground alone.

At present the insurance industry in the United Kingdom has two quite different Ombudsman schemes, one for life assurance and the other for non–life assurance. The schemes are differently constituted and make decisions on different principles; their respective enforcement mechanisms are also quite different. It is by no means uncommon to come upon policyholders who are confused as to the respective functions of the two schemes – there are each year some misdirected complaints. Moreover, it must be extremely difficult to explain to policyholders why the two schemes differ in their approaches,[49] even though there are apparently legitimate technical reasons for this. The position is in some ways simpler than it was before PIAOB, since in those days there were separate schemes for LAUTRO members, FIMBRA members and IOB members. Nevertheless, in terms of making the process reasonably transparent, reasonably comprehensible to policyholders, consistent and rational, there is urgent need to impose some degree of harmonisation within the various financial services Ombudsman schemes in the United Kingdom. This harmonisation might reasonably be undertaken as part of a broader process of harmonising complaints handling arrangements in financial services cases throughout Europe. With this in mind the next section now reviews the schemes currently in place in other Member States.

C.   Ombudsman Schemes Elsewhere in Europe

The concept of Ombudsman schemes originated in Scandinavia[50] though in the public sector rather than the private sector. It has, however, spread to the private sector in most countries of the European Union, and it is common to find that insurance is one of the sectors which has some kind of Ombudsman scheme.

The following summary shows the insurance Ombudsman schemes currently operating in EU Member States other than the United Kingdom.

---

49   A transitional problem which is still not entirely resolved is that the IOB continues to have a significant but decreasing backlog of financial services cases left over from the time before PIAOB came into existence.

50   'Ombudsman' is a Swedish word meaning 'grievance person'.

Denmark: The Insurance Complaints Board dates from 1975. It makes decisions in personal lines cases only (life and general), and only in cases involving disputes between a policyholder and his own insurer. Decisions are not binding on the policyholder, but are binding on the company unless it gives notice of objection within 30 days of the decision (something which happens in under 10% of cases). Complainants pay a modest fee when filing the case; this is refunded if they win or if the case is found to be outside the jurisdiction. In cases where the Board is unable to help, the Insurance Information Service can attempt to mediate between the parties, but this Service has no power to make binding decisions.

Finland: The Consumers Insurance Office dates from 1971, having been restructured in 1983. It deals with most types of personal lines insurance, but not with pension matters or with sickness or unemployment insurance. Its functions are limited to conciliation, as it has no power to make binding decisions in any case. In practice it appears that insurance companies usually comply with the recommendations of the Office, which take into account what is fair and reasonable as well as the strict legal position.

In addition to this general scheme, there are a number of more specialised *fora* to deal with particular types of insurance dispute. Areas covered by these schemes include traffic accidents and statutory accident insurance.

Sweden: The Consumers Insurance Office dates from 1979. The jurisdiction is mainly over personal lines policies, but commercial policies may also be considered provided that the policy in question is not essentially different from a personal lines policy. The Office gives advice to policyholders, the object of the scheme being to help policyholders to help themselves. This advice may involve taking the matter to court, but another possibility is to advise the policyholder to go to the insurance division of the General Consumer Complaints Board. Complaints must be lodged within six months of reaching deadlock with the company. The scheme is free to policyholders, but its conclusions act only as recommendations. In practice it appears that these recommendations are almost always complied with. Apart from this statutory scheme the Swedish insurance companies have set up a private complaints tribunal, composed of jurists and dealing with interpretation of policies and matters of basic principle in insurance law (but excluding life, accident and sickness policies). This system is entirely funded by the insurance industry and though it too makes no more than recommendations, those recommendations are almost always followed by the companies concerned. There is also a separate scheme for road traffic accident cases.

Eire: Since 1992 Eire has had an Insurance Ombudsman scheme similar to that operating in the United Kingdom. The scheme provides a free service to policyholders in personal lines cases (life and general), makes decisions which are binding on the insurance company and operates on the basis of what the Ombudsman considers fair and reasonable.

Germany: The federal Supervisory Board receives complaints concerning insurance companies, which it is obliged to investigate in order to obtain a reply for the complainant. However, the Board has no decision–making power, being limited to making recommendations.

Austria: There is no Ombudsman scheme, though the insurance companies have set up a scheme under which complaints can be made and submitted to the company for reconsideration.

Netherlands: The Netherlands has no fewer than four Ombudsman–type schemes. The most important is the non–Life Ombudsman, which dates from 1959 and is organised into specialised chambers for different types of non-life insurance. In addition to its responsive function of dealing with complaints, this scheme also has a pro–active jurisdiction to take up cases where it believes that insurers may have acted in such a way as to damage the reputation of the industry. Decisions in all cases are made on a fair and reasonable basis rather than according to strict legal rules.

The second scheme is a Life Assurance Ombudsman, dating from 1971, whilst the third, more specialised still and dating from 1983, deals only with life assurance based on mutual funds.

The fourth scheme deals with complaints about insurance marketing practices.

All four schemes are voluntary schemes funded and administered by the insurance industry. Although decisions are formally not binding on member companies, failure to comply is likely to lead to exclusion from the federation of Dutch insurers, a potential sanction which is apparently sufficient to ensure compliance in virtually all cases.

Belgium: There has been a scheme since 1983, operated and funded by the Association of Belgian Insurance Companies. The jurisdiction is limited to cases which are not already the subject of legal proceedings and which have not been submitted to the regulatory authorities. The scheme is limited to conciliation, having no power to make binding decisions.

Luxembourg: There is no specialised system for handling insurance-related complaints. However, it is possible to raise issues with the General Supervisory Authority, though this apparently has no decision–making power.

France: The position is very similar to that in Luxembourg. There is no specialist insurance Ombudsman system, and the national regulatory authorities cannot make binding decisions in individual cases, though they can act as conciliators, and their involvement in a given case is naturally likely to encourage the company to propose a reasonable settlement.

Italy: The National Insurance Association set up a claims office in 1977 to help policyholders in dealing with complaints against its members. The

Supervisory Authority also has a Complaints Division, set up in 1982. However, both of these have only a conciliatory role with no power to make binding decisions.

Portugal: There is no specialist insurance Ombudsman. The regulatory authorities can deal with complaints, but in addition there is an Ombudsman scheme of general application, whose powers include dealing with insurance matters.

Greece: There is no specialist insurance Ombudsman, though cases may be taken up with the regulatory authorities or with the Association of Insurance Companies, which will attempt to conciliate.

Spain: An Ombudsman scheme was introduced in 1995, though without binding powers.[51]

It is easy enough to identify a number of common, though not necessarily universal, features in these schemes. Most provide only advice and/or conciliation – the UK is unusual in having a scheme which can make decisions which bind the insurers. The evidence suggests that in most countries insurers comply with decisions even where these are not binding. On the other hand no country has a scheme in which complainants are bound. Most schemes are free to complainants, though a few do charge a modest fee.

D.   The Implications of Ombudsman Schemes for the Internal Market

Until now no serious thought appears to have been given to the question of how Ombudsman schemes are to be integrated into the development of the Internal Market in Insurance (or in financial services more generally). Why this is so must be a matter of speculation, but it is suggested that a plausible explanation lies in the voluntary character of many such schemes coupled with their tendency to be overburdened with work to the point where they are unable to look much beyond survival. Nevertheless, consideration of the question is overdue.

At the simplest level the issue may be posed in this way. Suppose that an insurer, exercising rights under the Single Passport System, sells a policy to a policyholder resident in a country other than that where the insurer has its headquarters (and therefore its Single Passport authorisation). Suppose also that the policyholder has a complaint about the way in which the policy was sold, or about its suitability or about some other aspect of the company's treatment of him. Does that policyholder have access to any Ombudsman scheme in an effort to obtain satisfaction of his grievance? If so, which

---

[51]   LEY 30/1995 of 8 November 1995, arts 61 and 63.

Ombudsman scheme? It hardly needs to be said that at the level of principle it is unacceptable for such a policyholder to be without the possibility of such redress, since that would imply that the cross–border nature of the transaction had put him at a disadvantage, thereby creating a disincentive to cross–border insurance, which would be contrary to the principles of the Internal Market. At the same time it is by no means easy to see which scheme would apply. At present all such schemes apply only to those who are members of them, even if membership is in some cases compulsory for some insurers or intermediaries. If the policyholder in the given case were in the United Kingdom but the insurer was not, the insurer would presumably not be a member of PIA and would not be a member of PIAOB. It is to be expected that the insurer would be a member of the Ombudsman scheme operating in its own country, but some such schemes, including IOB and PIAOB, are by their terms available only to policyholders resident in the country where the scheme operates. A rule of this kind necessarily creates a gap in the provision of Ombudsman redress, and it might well be thought that its obviously discriminatory character exposed it to challenge before the Court of Justice.

Even if this facet of the scheme were removed by allowing complaints to be brought by any policyholder who had purchased a policy from a member of the particular scheme, there would remain considerable practical difficulty for many policyholders, who would need to become familiar with the rules obtaining in another Member State and, presumably, would have to be able to correspond in the language of that State. A possible solution to this problem would be to provide that an insurer wishing to take advantage of the Single Passport by providing cross–border services would be required, when notifying the authorities of the host State of its intention, to submit to the jurisdiction of any relevant Ombudsman schemes operating in that State. This would accord with the general principles of both Ombudsman schemes and the regulatory legislation, both of which assume that the priority is to protect the policyholder, the insurer having enough resources and market power to be able to deal with the administrative and financial consequences of providing the necessary level of protection. The objection to this scheme is of course that it in effect adopts a scheme of host country regulation, when the whole thrust of the Directives is, for reasons discussed in Chapter 4, to adopt home country regulation. Although this statement is true as far as it goes, it does appear that this is one of the few areas where it is necessary to allow the retention of some residual degree of host country regulation. Ultimately, the only way in which this dilemma can be fully resolved is the same as the ultimate way of resolving all regulatory conflicts within the Internal Market, namely the creation of a single authority in Brussels. It was suggested in Chapter 4 that in a regulatory context such an outcome is not to be expected within the foreseeable future: the prospect seems, if anything, even more remote in the context of Ombudsman schemes, which vary greatly between Member States, the differences being much greater than those now experienced in regulatory systems. Perhaps a plausible interim measure would be to adopt a Directive on Complaints Handling in Insurance requiring every Member State to create a scheme which would adhere to certain basic principles of fairness, transparency, speed and equity.[52] The Code of Best Practice produced by the British and Irish Ombudsman Association could well be used as a starting point for the setting of appropriate standards. This could have the desirable effect of raising standards in many Member States as well as removing some of the disincentive to cross–border transactions by providing policyholders with an assurance of a reasonable level of protection. The foregoing comparison of existing schemes in different Member States identified a number of common features among those schemes, and it would seem possible to achieve a degree of harmonisation among the schemes. A very important question to be addressed is that of the binding character of decisions. The UK scheme may be regarded as offering better policyholder protection than any other, but it is somewhat out of line with the schemes in other Member States. It would seem desirable to adopt the usual EU practice of pursuing the highest possible level of consumer protection, and this would argue for a levelling up of standards by persuading other States to adopt the UK model. Given the power of the insurance lobby in most developed countries, however, this could prove somewhat difficult to achieve.

---

52   These are the major principles identified by the British and Irish Ombudsmans' Association working party on Best Practice.

6 The Competition Law Aspects[1]

In considering the role of EU competition law in the insurance sector, the first question to be addressed is whether the provisions of arts 85 and 86 apply at all within insurance. Prior to 1987 many in the insurance sector were prepared to argue that they did not,[2] alleging that these articles were relevant only in cases involving goods rather than services. In 1987 this argument was laid to rest and it was established that arts 85 and 86 TEU are in principle applicable to the insurance sector. This was established in *Verband der Sachsversicherer e V v Commission*[3] where the Court of Justice said:

> 'It must be concluded that the Community competition system, as set out in particular in Articles 85 and 86 EEC and in the provisions of Regulation 17, applies without restriction to the insurance industry.'

The Court made the point that derogations from the general application of arts 85 and 86 appear expressly in the Treaty in the relatively small number of cases where it is intended to grant such derogations, and there is no such general derogation for services, nor is there a more limited derogation for insurance or for financial services.

That case concerned the Association of Fire Insurers in Germany, which operated a system of making recommendations as to premiums to be charged by its members, though these recommendations were expressed to be non–binding. Following a period in which fire insurers had made losses for a number of years, the Association in 1980 issued various recommendations for premium increases. It was held that these recommendations were capable of breaching art. 85 as being a decision of an Association of undertakings,

---

1   Fitzsimmons, *Insurance Competition Law*, Graham Trotman, 1994; for a more general account of the competition law rules see Goyder, *EC Competition Law*, OUP, 1993.

2   Though some insurers, notably the P & I Clubs, had been prepared to operate on the assumption that it was applicable: See OJ 1985 L376/2 and Fitzsimmons, *The Application of EC Anti–Trust Law to the Insurance Industry*, in McGee and Heusel (eds), *The Law and Practice of Insurance in the Single European Market*, 1995 Bundesanzeiger.

3   [1987] ECR 405.

despite their non–binding character, because of the likelihood that they would have an anti–competitive effect. The Association's argument that it was merely trying to restore economic stability to the sector was rejected upon evidence that the recommendation was based on assumptions about standard levels of operating costs, even though in fact these showed significant variations from one company to another. Thus the Commission was entitled to conclude that the anti–competitive effects outweighed any likely benefit to consumers from the restoration of economic stability.

Once it is established that competition law rules are in principle applicable, it is next necessary to identify the two areas in which these rules are capable of having an impact. The first is that of anti–competitive practices by insurers themselves, whilst the second is that of national legislation in the sphere of insurance which might have anti–competitive effects.

1.   ANTI-COMPETITIVE PRACTICES

The problem of regulating competition in the insurance sector at EU level is to some extent the familiar one of discouraging the use of cartels and the abuse of monopoly power. From this point of view it might be said that the techniques to be used and the issues which arise are the same as those in any other sector of the market.

At the same time the insurance sector does exhibit some special features which might be thought to give rise to special problems. One important aspect of this is that in many Member States (though not the United Kingdom) there are systems of *ex ante* approval of policy terms. This leads to a considerable degree of uniformity between these terms and to the existence of a substantial body of common knowledge within the industry about insurance policies and practices. This is turn tends to lead to convergence of premiums and other terms and conditions, which is of course harmful to the development of free and vigorous competition.

In retrospect it is hard to see how the Court of Justice could have avoided concluding that the insurance sector is subject to the full force of the competition law provisions; to do so would inevitably have involved holding that all services fell outside these provisions, and it is clear that such a conclusion would have done irreparable damage to the Commission's attempts to develop the Internal Market as well as being inconsistent with the Court's normal purposive approach to the interpretation of Treaty provisions. However, such a conclusion does not by itself provide a satisfactory framework for the rational development of competition in the sector. Although art. 85(1) applies, art. 85(3) is in principle available to exempt particular agreements. In insurance, as in other sectors, the rather unpredictable operation of the system of individual exemptions[4] has understandably proved unpopular with many enterprises, and the question of Block Exemptions has therefore arisen. There are two Regulations which are relevant to this question. In the first of these, Regulation 1534/91 the Commission was authorised to create a Block Exemption covering a range of specified matters.

The matters in question were:

a. co–operation with respect to the establishment of common risk premium tariffs based on collectively ascertained statistics or the number of claims;
b. the establishment of common standard policy conditions;
c. the common coverage of certain types of risk;
d. the settlement of claims;
e. the testing and acceptance of security devices;
f. registers of, and information on, aggravated risks.

The Commission took advantage of this delegated power in the second of the two Regulations, Regulation 3932/92, though only in respect of four of the six areas which had been identified in the earlier Regulation, items (d) and (f) being for the moment omitted.

A. Common Risk Premium Tariffs

The purpose of this exemption is to allow insurers to share information relating to claims experience and other factors relevant to risk with a view to establishing what is sometimes referred to as the 'pure–risk premium', ie the amount which it would be necessary to charge simply in order to cover the risk, without any allowance for administration costs or for profit. The obtaining of better quality information on this point is likely to lead to more accurate premium calculation. However, the information thus obtained must be used purely for illustrative purposes. It is not permitted to have any agreement or concerted practice as to the level of premiums actually charged. Art. 3 of the Regulation imposes the detailed conditions for the applicability of this exemption. The calculations, tables or study results referred to in art. 2, when compiled and distributed, must include a statement that they are purely illustrative. The calculations or tables referred to in art. 2(a) must not include in any way loadings for contingencies, income deriving from reserves, administrative or commercial costs comprising commissions

---

4   Goyder, note 1 above.

payable to intermediaries, fiscal or para–fiscal contributions or the anticipated profits of the participating undertakings. The calculations, tables or study results referred to in art. 2 do not identify the insurance undertakings concerned.

Art. 4 then imposes a further restriction, namely that the exemption shall not benefit undertakings or associations of undertakings which enter into an undertaking or commitment among themselves or which oblige other undertakings, not to use calculations or tables which differ from those established pursuant to art. 2(a) or not to depart from the results of the studies referred to in art. 2(b).

B.   Common Standard Policy Conditions

Standard policy conditions for direct insurance and standard models which illustrate the profits of a life assurance policy can be exempted from art. 85. They must be established and distributed with a statement that they are purely illustrative. They must expressly mention the possibility that different terms may be agreed and the standard terms must be accessible to anyone on request in order to promote transparency of information.

In a UK context it is interesting to note that projections as to the returns to be obtained on investment policies are already required to conform to principles laid down by the Personal Investment Authority.[5] Since these principles include details of the investment returns to be assumed (a lower and a higher rate of return being specified) it follows that for any given type of policy the projected returns will be the same whichever insurer is involved. This rule was introduced as part of the 1986 reform of financial services law,[6] and the rationale for it was the desire to prevent insurers from issuing projections showing absurdly inflated returns, accompanied by a notice in small print showing that these returns were projected but not guaranteed. It was considered, no doubt rightly, that prospective policyholders would not be willing to buy investment policies without at least some indication of what returns might be expected, and the compromise solution reached was to require a standard set of projections, giving a lower and higher rate of return, accompanied by a clear and visible notice that there are no guarantees as to the returns actually obtained, which may not fall within the range indicated in the projections. It may be doubted whether this is particularly helpful to prospective policyholders, who are still left with only the vaguest of ideas of what the return will be, but it is hard to rebut the argument that in the nature

---

5   Financial Services Act 1986, as amended.

6   Financial Services Act 1986.

of investment policies there can be no guarantee as to the eventual return. In the present context, however, the more important point must be that these rules are by their nature anti–competitive to the extent that they prevent individual insurers from obtaining a commercial advantage by offering more optimistic projections. The rule is of course not subject to art. 85, being imposed by law rather than having its origins in the behaviour of commercial undertakings. Moreover, it is a relatively easy matter to justify the rule as being necessary for the protection of consumers, since its effect is to prevent the making of overly optimistic projections which do not then come true. There is no advantage to consumers in allowing them to be misled by inaccurate projections. It would of course be a different matter if the information given related not to projections but to guaranteed minimum returns. In practice there are very few instances where this is the case. One of the rare exceptions occurs where an endowment policy sold in connection with a mortgage is guaranteed to be adequate to pay off the mortgage at the end of the term of the policy.

C.   Common Coverage of Certain Types of Risk

This exemption applies to agreements which aim to set up and operate groups of insurers, or insurers and re–insurers for the common coverage of a specific category of risks in the form of co–insurance or re–insurance. This aspect of the Block Exemption Regulation is intended to encourage co–operation in those areas where for technical reasons it is difficult to find individual insurers who are willing to take on the risk. Art. 10 goes on to detail the matters which may be covered by the agreement. Art. 11 then imposes a further very important restriction by providing that the exemption does not apply to a co–insurance group which has more than 10% of the relevant market or to a co–reinsurance group which has more than 15% of the relevant market. However, in some cases the limits apply only to products brought within the group and subject to its rules; they do not apply to identical products marketed by a member of the group but not brought within the group where the products cover catastrophe risks for which the claims are by their nature both large and rare or where the products relate to aggravated risks, ie those which by the nature of the risk involve a higher probability of claims.[7] In all other cases the limits apply to all products of the relevant class provided by members of the group, whether they are brought within the group or not.

---

[7]   Art. 11.2.

(i)   Testing and Acceptance of Security Devices

Art. 14 of the Block Exemption Regulation confers exemption on agreements, decisions and concerted practices intended to promote the establishment, recognition and distribution of technical specifications for security devices, as well as procedures for assessing whether particular security devices comply with the technical specifications and for dealing with the installation and maintenance of such devices.

Art. 15 of the Regulation goes on to impose further detailed conditions for the application of this exemption. These are as follows:

The technical specifications and compliancy assessment procedures must be precise, technically justified and in proportion to the performance to be attained by the security device concerned.

The rules for the evaluation of installation undertakings and maintenance undertakings must be objective, must relate to their technical competence and must be applied in a non-discriminatory manner.

Such specifications and rules must be established and distributed with the statement that insurance undertakings are free to accept other security devices or approve other installation and maintenance undertakings which do not comply with these technical specifications or rules.

Such specifications and rules must be provided simply upon request to any interested person and must include a classification based on the level of performance obtained.

Any applicant must be free to submit a request for assessment at any time and the evaluation of conformity must not impose on the applicant expenses disproportionate to the costs of the approval procedure.

The devices and installation and maintenance undertakings which meet the assessment criteria must be certified to that effect (in writing) in a non-discriminatory manner within a period of six months of the date of application, except where technical considerations justify a reasonable additional period.

The grounds for a refusal to issue a certificate of compliance must be stated in writing by attaching a duplicate copy of the records of the tests and controls that have been carried out.

The grounds for a refusal to take into account a request for assessment must be stated in writing.

The specifications and rules must be applied by bodies observing the appropriate provisions of norms in the series EN 45 000.

(ii) Non–Compliant Practices

In the case of an agreement or concerted practice which does not fall within the Block Exemption, the parties are still required to notify the Commission, but may apply for individual exemption under art. 85(3). An application of this kind will be determined according to the normal principles applied to art. 85(3) cases. Given that the Regulation does not deal with all the areas authorised to be covered by the earlier Regulation 1534/91, and given that the Commission's work in this area is obviously far from complete, it seems to be much too soon to say that there will be a presumption against the granting of art. 85(3) exemption to agreements which do not fall within the terms of the Block Exemption.

(iii) Withdrawal of the Exemption

In art. 17 of the Regulation the Commission reserves to itself the power to withdraw the benefit of the exemption in a particular case if it appears that the operation of the exemption is having undesirable anti–competitive effects. In particular (but without limitation) this applies to premium calculations where the studies used as the basis for the calculation are based on unjustifiable hypotheses, to standard policy conditions which create a significant imbalance between the rights and obligations under the contract and to common coverage agreements where the undertakings concerned could easily compete in the market on their own, where one or more of the participating undertakings has a determining influence on the commercial policy of more than one group, where the setting up of the group results in the sharing of the market for the products concerned and where a group has such a position with regard to aggravated risks that policyholders encounter considerable difficulty in obtaining cover outside the group.

So far there is no reported case of the Commission seeking to withdraw the benefit of the exemption in any given case. Indeed, as the Commission admits in the Green Book of May 1996,[8] experience of the operation of the Regulation is to date very limited. It therefore seems appropriate to attempt to address at the level of principle some of the issues relating to competition in the insurance sector across the European Union.

It is a commonplace to say that arts 85 and 86 are built on the notion that the 'ideal' state of the market for any given product is that which is known to economists as 'perfect competition', in which all parties have complete information about all products available, price is determined purely

---

[8] For detailed discussion of the Green Book see Chapter 7.

by the mechanics of supply and demand and no one buyer or seller has enough market share or power to exercise significant influence on the behaviour of any other party. This is of course a highly idealised description of a market–place, bearing only passing resemblance to any commonly encountered, but that should not and does not prevent the Commission from constantly striving to get as near to such a market as can be achieved.

In the case of the insurance sector it can be seen that there are a number of very significant practical obstacles to achieving this market structure. First, this is a market in which all the sellers are large organisations, whilst virtually all the buyers (all in the area of personal lines insurance) are private individuals with no significant market power. Second, there is by no means perfect information among buyers. There are many sellers, and, at least in the United Kingdom, the products they offer are numerous and different from each other in subtle but important ways. Moreover, those ways are often by no means apparent even on an initial reading of the relevant policies, for it is another commonplace of the insurance market that policies (especially investment policies) are written in language almost incomprehensible to the non–expert. Another important feature of the market is the extreme importance of the product in a significant number of cases. There are those areas where insurance is compulsory (motor insurance being the most important example) as well as areas such as pension provision, which is commonly effected through insurance policies, and which, even if not compulsory, is fundamental to the life planning of most citizens. The essential nature of insurance creates a situation in which most people are more or less forced to buy a policy at some time, even though they may understand little or nothing of the relevant law or of the workings of the insurance market. This only serves to increase the imbalance between sellers and buyers. The next important feature of the market, at least in the area of personal lines policies, is the more or less universal employment of standard form policies. Insurance is essentially a volume business, using standard forms which are issued very rapidly to large numbers of customers. Although it is not impossible to negotiate for special terms to cover particular risks, this is relatively rarely done, and the typical insurance broker is not alert to the possibility that an individual client may have special needs.

The account of the market given so far might well lead an observer to suppose that there were no circumstances in which any kind of anti–competitive agreement or concerted practice among insurers could possibly be justified. Such a conclusion would, however, be premature. Insurance is of course all about risk, and in the long run the thing most conducive to the perpetuation of efficient, economically viable insurance across the widest possible range of activity is good information about risk, ie good risk assessment data. Poor data will result either in excessive premiums, to the detriment of consumers, or in inadequate premiums, with the result that the insurer will not survive long in the market. The Commission is still to a considerable extent feeling its way in establishing which information–sharing and other practices are likely in reality to have anti–competitive effects. In looking at the market for insurance, it may well still be necessary to distinguish quite sharply between different Member States. Certainly, a consideration of the position in the UK would tend to lead to the conclusion that the market is highly competitive, with many different policies and with new products entering the market on a regular basis. This situation is of course in part a reflection of the absence of any system for *ex ante* approval of policies in the UK, and this is a major reason why the position may be different elsewhere. A second important reason for the fluid nature of the UK market is the continuing over–capacity, which has been identified elsewhere[9] as a cause of other long–term problems in the regulation of the industry. The former of these two features is certainly absent in most other Member States, and it appears that the latter may also be absent, in which case the risk of anti–competitive practices is much greater. On the other hand, there have so far apparently been no cases in which the Commission has imposed fines on insurance undertakings for breaches of art. 85 or art. 86.

(iv) National Legislation

There have been two reported cases in which the compatibility of national insurance–related legislation with art. 85 has been considered. In the case of Meng[10] the Court dealt with a rule prohibiting intermediaries from transferring to their clients all or part of the commission which they received from insurance companies for the placing of business. Although such a rule is clearly capable of having anti–competitive effects, it was held that it does not infringe art. 85. The same result was reached in the case of Ohra[11] where the rule in question forbade insurance undertakings from granting collateral advantages (such as credit cards) to clients or beneficiaries of insurance policies. Here the Court simply followed the reasoning in the case of Meng, both judgments being delivered on the same day.

The obvious difficulty about the application of art. 85 in such cases is that the rules in question were rules of the national legislation, rather than concerted practices in the private sector. However, the Court has consistently held that Member States have an obligation to ensure that their national legislation does not contain rules which would undermine the effect of the

---

9   See Chapters 1 and 8.

10   Case C–2/91 OJ 1994 C/1/1314; [1994] ECR I/ 5751.

11   Case C–245/91 [1993] ECR I/5851.

competition law provisions. It was therefore necessary to examine the substance of these provisions to see whether they had that effect. The Court in these cases took a somewhat narrow view of the prohibition on undermining competition law. It said that national rules could have this effect if, but only if, they either required the adoption by private sector organisations of anti–competitive rules or consolidated such rules where they already existed, The former requirement was obviously not satisfied. Since the adoption of rules by private sector organisations was simply not in point – the anti–competitive restrictions imposed by the national laws were mandatory. The question of consolidation of existing anti–competitive practices proved more difficult. The Commission alleged that practices of this kind had grown up before the national legislation, which had simply embodied them into domestic law, but the Court found that this was not proved. Presumably the decision would have gone the other way if the Commission had been able to substantiate its allegations. This illustrates the distinctly unsatisfactory nature of the distinction drawn in these cases. The nature and effect of the restrictions is the same whether or not they consolidate pre–existing practices, yet the Court allows this to be the vital distinction on which the applicability of art. 85 turns. It is submitted that the restrictions in question were clearly undesirable and that their existence did undermine the effectiveness of art. 85. The effect of the decisions is therefore to allow the entrenchment of anti–competitive practices (and not just in the insurance sector). On the basis of these decisions it is not surprising that there has so far been no effective challenge under arts 85 and 86 to restrictive legislation in the insurance sector.

7 The Commission's Review

The implementation deadline for the Third Directives was 1 July 1994, so the Single Passport system has, at least in theory,[1] been in force for a little over three years. The Commission has monitored the progress of the law and practice of the Single Passport system, and in May 1996 it produced a Green Book summarising its findings.[2]

The Green Book takes as its starting point the need for legislation in the insurance sector to provide proper protection for the interests of consumers. The various Directives considered in earlier Chapters are of course primarily aimed at the providers of services, since they are with only a few exceptions directed at regulation rather than at insurance contract law.[3] Nevertheless, the interests of consumers are not entirely neglected, for the Directives do contain provisions dealing with the questions of giving consumers full and accurate information before the contract is entered into,[4] protecting their legal interests[5] and ensuring that they have access to methods of recourse in the case of dispute.[6] It might also be said that the detailed provisions of the Directives on minimum capital and rules of conduct are aimed at the protection of consumers by helping to raise the quality and stability of insurers.

The Commission goes on to identify what it presently sees as the most pressing and serious problems from the point of view of consumers in the functioning of the Internal Market in Insurance. These are refusal by some insurers to provide services to non–residents, failure to provide policyholders with adequate information and the fraudulent conduct of some unscrupulous intermediaries. The Commission also draws attention to the questions arising

---

1   See Chapter 1 for the history of the implementation of these Directives in different Member States.

2   Com (96) 209 *Services financiers; Repondre aux attentes des consommateurs*, May 1996.

3   The conspicuous exception is the Draft Directive on Insurance Contract Law, discussed in Chapter 5, though this never became law.

4   Art. 31 of both the Third Life and Third non–Life Directives; it may be noted that this would have been more effectively achieved by the enactment of art. 2 of the 1979 Draft Directive on Insurance Contract Law, more fully discussed in Chapter 5.

5   *Ibid.*

6   *Ibid.*

from the practice of distance selling. These four major areas are considered in more detail below.

1.   REFUSAL TO PROVIDE SERVICES TO NON-RESIDENTS

The Green Book recites evidence presented to the Commission of individual insurers refusing to provide insurance (it is not clear whether this is life or non–life business) to persons who are not resident within the same Member State as the insurer. The Green Book makes the obvious point that this practice appears to be quite incompatible with all notions of European integration, the Internal Market and with the most basic principles of non-discrimination. Clearly such conduct cannot be tolerated in an Internal Market.

However, the inadequate account of these cases given in the Green Book raises a number of fascinating questions in the mind of the reader, and it is not possible to comment sensibly on the general question of refusal to insure without knowing the answers to at least some of them.

First, it would be desirable to know which types of insurance are involved here. At the most basic level it would be useful to know whether these problems have arisen in life or non–life business. Within non–life business it is suggested that there might be significant differences between, for example, motor insurance, liability insurance and the insurance of property (real or personal). Underlying the wish for this knowledge is an awareness that the problem of refusal to insure cannot be properly tackled without knowing why in any given case an insurer apparently declines available business. In the absence of proper evidence it is not possible to do more than speculate, but it is suggested that various reasons can be imagined for refusal to insure. Perhaps the most obvious example arises in relation to motor insurance. In this sector a major factor determining the claims experience for any insurer is the incidence of liability for accidents. This in turn depends on the details of the law of tort/delict in the country concerned, and an insurer not familiar with the details of other countries' laws may feel inhibited in calculating appropriate premiums. Moreover, an insurer's prospects of being able to negotiate satisfactory settlements in disputed cases (of which there are likely to be many) will depend upon a familiarity with the customs and practices of the national market and to an extent the behaviour of individual insurance companies. It is easy to see that the acquisition costs of the necessary expertise and know–how are considerable, so that some insurers may feel reluctant to plunge into this sector of the market. As against that there is some anecdotal evidence of insurance companies being willing to provide motor insurance to its own expatriate citizens, especially those who are posted abroad by their employers. It seems that one of the most common instances of this occurs in the case of nationals who are sent to work in Belgium or Luxembourg for one or other of the institutions of the European Union. It may well be thought appropriate that this circumstance should provide a testing ground for the operation of the Internal Market in motor insurance.

In the case of property insurance, where liability to third parties is less likely to be in issue (though some policies will include public liability cover) the reluctance to become involved is less easy to understand. In the case of buildings policies, it may be that the special conditions of the housing market in particular countries are a concern to some insurers. This is particularly easy to imagine in the case of the United Kingdom, where a very large proportion of personal lines buildings policies are in fact sold in conjunction with a mortgage, the holding of such a policy being usually a condition of the mortgage. Because of this many such policies are in fact constructed as block policies held by the mortgagee for the benefit of the mortgagee and the mortgagor. Mortgagees, who will normally be very large commercial organisations with substantial market power, then insist on favourable terms as to price, as well as considerable protection from the avoidance of the policy in the case of non–disclosure by an individual home–owner. These peculiarities in the market are of course a consequence of the very high proportion of owner–occupied homes found in the United Kingdom, a feature which is not at all prevalent in other Member States. It can be seen that this is another example of cultural differences which might discourage insurers from providing cross–border services. It might justly be added, however, that in the case of the United Kingdom an insurance company which did wish to enter this market might find it far from easy to do so, since mortgagees normally insist that their borrowers insure with an insurer approved by them. Increasingly, the approved insurers will turn out to be a captive subsidiary of the mortgagee; even where this is not so, mortgagees will try to direct the business towards a limited panel of insurers with whom they have established satisfactory (to them) relationships.[7] Breaking into this established market is likely to be difficult.

In the case of life policies issues of a different kind might arise. The difficulty relates not so much to term assurance, the purest form of life assurance with no endowment or investment element, as to investment policies. This is an area where existing national rules may in some cases make the selling of policies across national boundaries extremely difficult if not impossible. As in a number of other cases the United Kingdom appears

---

[7]   Though the Building Societies Ombudsman has ruled that Building Society mortgagees must accept other insurers chosen by mortgagors provided that they offer suitable policies – Annual Report 1993–94.

to present some significant problems. Although authorisation to sell such policies in the United Kingdom, as anywhere else in the European Union, would have to depend on home State authorisation, the position is apparently different when it comes to the control of the selling and marketing of policies. In this area the United Kingdom's rules are derived from the Financial Services Act 1986. These are of a very detailed character, with many restrictions and requirements as to the content of advertising material, the use of intermediaries (the United Kingdom is alone in the European Union in adopting the concept of polarisation) and selling practices. It is easy to imagine why an insurer in another Member State might be unwilling to become involved in selling investment policies in the United Kingdom.

The three examples chosen to illustrate reasons for possible refusal to sell insurance on a cross–border basis may also be taken to demonstrate a more general point about the Internal Market in Insurance. This is that residual legal differences and, most of all, cultural differences, may well lead insurers to decline to take advantage of the apparent freedom offered to them by the new regime. It is to be hoped that the enquiries currently being undertaken by the Commission into the functioning of the Internal Market in general will help to identify which of these possible obstacles are in fact operating in the insurance sector.

2.   FAILURE TO PROVIDE ADEQUATE INFORMATION

The 1979 Draft Directive on Insurance Contract Law would have imposed requirements as to the information to be given to the policyholder at the time the contract was entered into, though of course this never became law. In the United Kingdom the Financial Services Act 1986 imposes extensive requirements as to information to be provided to prospective policyholders in the case of investment policies. In any event an examination of the documentation which is in practice provided with general policies in the United Kingdom would scarcely support the notion that this country has a problem with failure to provide adequate information. It may of course be that the position is quite different in other Member States.

3.   FRAUD BY INTERMEDIARIES

In this area the Green Book identifies only a limited area of concern, namely the selling of policies by unauthorised and thus unregulated intermediaries. It is not clear where in the European Union this practice is a serious problem. Certainly it is not encountered with any regularity in the United Kingdom. On the other hand, the United Kingdom does suffer from very serious problems in relation to the activities of intermediaries, though the Green Book does not allude to these at all. Historically the standards of competence and honesty of insurance intermediaries in the United Kingdom have been very low, there being no tradition of professional standards or approach in this area. The Financial Services Act 1986 made an attempt to address these issues by imposing the concept of polarisation and by setting up Self-Regulating Organisations to control the activities of product providers (LAUTRO) and of independent intermediaries (FIMBRA). Despite the endeavours of these organisations the late 1980s and early 1990s saw misselling of personal pension policies on a massive scale, as well as continued misselling of other insurance–based products. At the same time the number of independent intermediaries fell dramatically. In 1994 the system was reformed by merging LAUTRO and FIMBRA into a single organisation, the Personal Investment Authority, whose remit is to cover all forms of personal (ie non–business) investment.[8] One of the first acts of the PIA was to order a major review of the selling of pensions policies since 1988, when the new–style personal pension plans first became available. This review is ongoing, and it has been estimated that it could cost the insurance industry as much as £2 billion to correct the consequences of the misselling of pensions since 1988. In the Spring of 1997, with the existing Pensions Review not complete, the government announced proposals for fundamental reforms to the state retirement pension, one effect of which would be to require virtually all adults to take out private pensions. Those who have watched the misselling of the past ten years and its consequences may be forgiven for feeling some alarm at the prospect of the sale of very large numbers of pension policies to very unsophisticated investors.

Although the misselling of pensions has, at least in the United Kingdom, tended to overshadow all other issues of insurance misselling in recent years, it should be remembered that there are also other cases of misselling in relation to investment policies, and that at least some of these examples are ongoing. For example, in the mid–1980s, a time of high and rising property values, it became fashionable for insurance companies to offer what were called Home Income Plans, a scheme under which elderly homeowners were invited to release a portion of the capital value of their homes by taking out mortgages, on which they paid only the interest, the intention being that the capital released would in whole or in part be invested in the company's own funds. The promotional literature suggested that in the prevailing conditions of strong Stock Market growth the rising income from this investment could be used to pay the interest on the mortgage and still leave a surplus for the

---

8   Though savings and deposit accounts are not investments for these purposes – Financial Services Act 1986, Schedule 1.

mortgagors (whilst of course also leaving a modest profit for the insurance company). The scheme was fraught with the obvious danger that the income from the invested loan would be or become insufficient even to meet the mortgage payments. This was likely to happen if ever the growth of the Stock Market slowed significantly. Since it is well known that Stock Market growth is neither predictable nor steady, and that all such markets undergo periods of decline and retrenchment, it was foreseeable at the outset that Home Income Plans would at some stage encounter this difficulty. Considerable amounts of time and money have since been expended in rectifying the misselling of Home Income Plans. Despite this in the Summer of 1996 a number of well-known companies again began selling this type of policy, still under the name Home Income Plan. No great prescience is needed in order to see that within the next five years or so many of the same problems will recur unless very great care is taken in the selling of these policies. The history of the industry in this regard does not give much grounds for expecting the taking of such care.

The continued high level of cases of misselling[9] by intermediaries in the United Kingdom raises a number of interesting issues when considered from a European perspective. The first question is whether misselling of this kind is as prevalent in other Member States. The absence of this issue from the Green Book leads to the suspicion that the United Kingdom is the most serious offender in this category. If that suspicion is correct, it is necessary to ask why this is so. Although the adoption of the concept of polarisation has been heavily criticised, it must be said that the position appears to have been no better under the pre-1986 law, so that it is difficult to make a convincing case that polarisation has been a significant contributory factor. Indeed, it is very hard to identify with any conviction just why this is such a problem in the United Kingdom. The existence of over-capacity in the insurance market, coupled with the longstanding use of the commission system, may go some way towards providing an explanation. The really interesting question, though, is whether the problem of misselling is prevalent elsewhere and, if it is, whether it is accompanied by over-capacity and the commission system.

Whatever the answers to these major questions, the Commission is going to have to consider what steps, if any, it can take to tackle undesirable behaviour by intermediaries. The tone of the Green Book does not encourage optimism on this score, since the Commission's present belief appears to be that matters of this kind can only properly be regulated by national

---

9   As evidenced, for example, by the continued high level of complaints to the Insurance Ombudsman Bureau and now the Personal Investment Authority Ombudsman Bureau.

authorities. In fact, this view is quite misplaced, and the existing experience of raising standards of conduct and competence by action at European level should offer a useful guide as to the way to proceed. The difficulty appears to be that national legislation still does not impose proper requirements of professionalism. Although, at least in the UK, those wishing to be insurance intermediaries, whether acting for product providers or for purchasers of insurance-based products, have to be authorised by the Personal Investment Authority, the standards applied to those seeking such authorisation still do not appear to be very high. Certainly, it cannot be said that insurance intermediaries have reached the status of a profession, for despite the entry requirements and ongoing authorisation requirements (with the possibility of loss of authorisation for those whose behaviour is seen to fall below the acceptable standard) one of the fundamental aspects of a profession, namely the rule that in all circumstances the professional must put the interests of the client before his own interests, is still conspicuously absent. It is suggested that there can be no question of professional status until this rule is adopted. The role of the Commission in developing better standards of conduct is to treat the question of harmonisation of standards for intermediaries with the same seriousness as has been applied to the harmonisation of standards for the insurers themselves. The next step is therefore a proper Insurance Intermediaries Directive, requiring Member States to adapt their domestic laws to conform to minimum standards. The emphasis of these minimum standards should be consumer protection, and to this end it should become compulsory to require intermediaries to behave in the professional way already described.

4.   DISTANCE SELLING

There is already a draft Distance Selling Directive,[10] though after some discussion the draft adopted by the European Parliament has specifically excluded financial services from the scope of the Directive on the ground that the issues in financial services are too complex to be adequately addressed in a Directive intended to be of general application.

Two obvious points may be made. First, it is far from clear that this proposition is true. Second, even if it is true, there is still a pressing need to address the issues of the distance selling of financial services, even if it takes a specifically dedicated Directive to achieve that objective.

The truth of the claim that financial services cannot be dealt with in a general Directive (a claim which the Green Book makes but does not justify

---

[10]   OJ 30.10.95 C288.

by any kind of rational argument) must depend on showing that financial services have some special characteristics, relevant to the issue of distance selling. It is not clear what these might be. It is true that for many years financial services have been sold at a distance as well as face–to–face, but that applies to many other products, including the very large ranges of goods which are commonly sold by mail order as well as being available in the shops. On the other hand, it might be said that the analogy with the sale of goods is misplaced, since services cannot so readily be returned if they prove unsuitable, even assuming that in the case of financial services it can be clearly decided what is and is not suitable. Indeed, it is probably fair to say that services are relatively rarely sold at a distance, not least because many services have to be delivered on the purchaser's premises (which is not true of insurance services). It may then be appropriate to have separate Directives (or perhaps just separate provisions in a single Directive) dealing with goods and services respectively.

Since it is clear, whatever the merits of the first argument, that provisions are needed to deal with the distance selling of insurance, it may be helpful to look at the draft Distance Selling Directive in order to understand at least some of the issues which arise and to glean some idea of the Commission's present thinking in this area.

5. CONSTITUTIONAL ASPECTS OF THE COMMISSION'S BEHAVIOUR

Some commentators have raised the question of the constitutionality of the Commission's behaviour in announcing its own interpretations of the Directives and Regulations. It has been suggested that in this way the Commission is in effect arrogating legislative power to itself.

Clearly, there is a fine dividing line between interpreting and applying the law, on the one hand, and effectively changing the law by announcing interpretations which cannot reasonably be justified according to the wording of the legislation in question. The Commission is compelled to do the former of these – indeed it is the Commission's duty to do it as part of its function of guardian of the Treaties and developer of the Internal Market. On the other hand, it is clearly not legitimate for it to do the second of these things, since that usurps the legislative function of the Council. Unfortunately, the distinction, though easy to state, is rather more difficult to apply, since there will inevitably be cases where the proper interpretation of the legislation is open to considerable dispute. In such cases a particular interpretation may be regarded by one observer as a legitimate exercise of the Commission's functions but by another as a usurpation of legislative power. At the level of principle the only possible solution to this dilemma is to accord the

Commission the power to make and issue interpretations, subject to a right of appeal to the Court by persons aggrieved. This is certainly an area where the Commission needs to tread carefully.

6. THE INSURANCE COMMITTEE

The Insurance Committee was created by Directive 91/675/EEC with effect from 1 January 1992. It consists of representatives of the Member States and its job is to assist the Commission on its work in the insurance sector. Before taking any measures in the insurance sector, the Commission must consult the Committee.[11] If the Committee approves the proposed measures, the Commission must adopt them. Otherwise the Commission submits the proposals to the Council, which may adopt them by qualified majority vote.[12]

The Committee is prohibited from considering issues relating to individual insurance companies.[13]

The Committee functions in effect as specialist expert support for the work of the Commission, and its approval can be sufficient to cause the Commission to adopt proposed measures (though it does not have a right of veto). The Committee is not, however, a forum for the expression of the views of interested parties other than the Member States, since neither the industry nor the consumers are represented on it.

7. OTHER AREAS OF CONCERN

The Green Book is written entirely from the point of view of the need to protect consumers. This is obviously an important aspect of the Commission's work, but it cannot be considered to be the only significant issue when reviewing the development of the Single Market under the Third Directives regime. It is also necessary to consider the position of the insurance undertakings. For them the advent of the Single Market on 1 July 1994 should have brought new opportunities in the sense that the right of establishment throughout the EU was properly recognised, but also new threats in the sense that no national market could any longer be protected from incursions by undertakings from other Member States. In the long run the logic of this ought to be that there would be considerable interpenetration

---

11   Art 2.
12   *Ibid.*
13   Art. 3(2).

of national markets to the advantage of consumers and efficient businesses (though this would be accompanied by the natural free market corollary that inefficient businesses could expect to suffer and perhaps even to fail entirely). It must be said, however, that to date very little of this seems to have happened, at least in the United Kingdom. As far as is known, no major insurer from another Member State has made any serious attempt to achieve a market share by direct marketing to consumers. This sector of the general insurance market is dominated by five very large composite insurers[14] with well–established marketing techniques and practices. In the life and investment sector there are rather more large players, though the same five still dominate. It will not be at all easy for any existing UK insurer to break that dominance, far less for any non UK insurer with all the difficulties of language and culture which such an undertaking would face. It is therefore perhaps not surprising to find that the major development seen so far in the UK has been that a number of major undertakings have entered into strategic alliances with undertakings in other Member States; these have generally taken the form of the two undertakings concerned acquiring substantial[15] minority shareholdings in each other. This scheme effectively allows them to share to a limited and carefully controlled extent in each other's fortunes without requiring either to develop new products or tackle new markets. The attractions of such a scheme to the undertakings are obvious, but it is equally obvious that these agreements are capable of having anti–competitive effects: even if there is no formal agreement that the undertakings concerned will not enter each other's territory (and a formal agreement to this effect would surely breach art. 85) it is in practice likely that an undertaking which has entered into such an arrangement will find it commercially undesirable to compete in this way, so that an anti–competitive effect will be achieved. It would therefore seem that such agreements must in principle be capable of infringing art. 85. Moreover, the development of a network of such agreements among major insurers in different Member States is almost bound to have such an anti–competitive effect, even if each individual agreement is purely bi–lateral. To date the Commission has not taken any step towards dealing with such arrangements, and, so far as is known, there are no networks of bi–lateral agreements. It may be that to date there have been too few such agreements to constitute a serious problem, or that the undertakings involved have not been large enough to attract the attention of the Commission, though the latter point may be doubted, given that

---

14   Royal Sun Alliance, Prudential, Legal and General, General Accident and Commercial Union.

15   Usually about 20%.

Commercial Union was among the UK insurers entering into at least one such arrangement.

It is clear that there is a major potential issue here. If the existence of the Single Market does not in fact lead to the greater interpenetration and competition which should be its natural consequences, then the time will inevitably come when the Commission begins to ask difficult questions about what features of this sector of the market are precluding those developments. At that point, if not before, these strategic alliances are likely to receive considerable critical attention.

8.   THE NEXT STEP

In conclusion the Commission accepts that the information which it has in its possession on the functioning of the Internal Market in insurance is as yet only fragmentary, mainly because the Green Book was published less than two years after the implementation date of the Third Directives. The Green Book therefore invites interested parties to provide further information and comments as part of a more general debate, the aim of which is to identify more accurately the priority areas for further action. It is to be hoped that these areas will not be limited to matters of direct concern to the consumer lobby, but will extend to considering the needs and legitimate interests of the insurance undertakings. Possible future developments are considered more fully in the next chapter.

8 The Future

The future of the Internal Market in insurance cannot be considered in isolation. It is inevitably closely linked to at least two other issues, one narrow and one broad. The narrow issue is how the financial services sector as a whole will develop within the Europe of the future, a form of words which itself conceals many very difficult issues about the future shape of the European Union. The broader issue concerns the development of the Internal Market as a whole within the same imprecisely defined 'future Europe'. Within these two large questions there are other more detailed issues about the roles of the various players, namely the financial institutions in the broadest sense, the regulatory authorities of Member States and the Commission.

1. FUTURE EUROPE

This is perhaps the most important of all the issues considered in this chapter and certainly the most difficult. At the time of writing it is unclear whether the trend towards greater integration implicit in the Maastricht Treaty will ever be realised or whether notions of subsidiarity (or even of blatant national self–interest) will become more important and powerful, resulting in a weakening of the links within the European Union. It is also unclear who will be the Member States of that Union in ten years' time. Currently, there are numerous applicants for membership, and the Commission continues to talk of a further expansion in the year 2000, though it is not clear that this is possible, either practically or politically.

The importance of a possible further expansion for the development of the Internal Market cannot be overstated. There have been for many years past two major strands of development within the European Union. For convenience these may be referred to as *broadening* and *deepening*. Broadening implies an increase in the membership of the European Union, whereas deepening implies the development of closer links between member states, including a closer degree of political, economic, legal and even social and cultural union. The difficulty is to choose which of these two objectives to prioritise. The diplomatic answer to this question is to say that both are essential and must be pursued vigorously. Unfortunately, this answer ignores the essential point that the two objectives are to some extent in conflict. The pursuit of deepening assumes that there is already a considerable base of common ground among the Member States, ie that all, or virtually all,

Member States are at a roughly similar point in their development, and that the task is to build on this base. This assumption is perhaps more or less true of the existing fifteen Member States, though even among these States the discrepancies in levels of prosperity and economic development are substantial; the very existence of the Regional Development Fund and the designation of particular areas as qualifying for Priority Assistance may be seen as ample testimony to that proposition. The differences in levels of development are of course very much more acute when the potential Eastern European members of the EU are considered. Even in the more advanced of those countries – Poland, Hungary, Czechia and the Slovak Republic – economic development lags well behind that in the present European Union, and the legal systems of these countries are still grappling with the transition from the pre–1989 Communist regimes. Although the Commission's PHARE Programme is leading to the making of very serious efforts by these countries to raise the level of development and sophistication of their systems in preparation for possible entry into the European Union, it seems inevitable that their entry will result either in the slowing down of the deepening programme generally or in the granting to these countries of extensive derogations from the general Internal Market rules for periods well beyond the normal twelve–year transition period accorded to new members. These observations point to the conclusion that for sometime to come broadening is likely to be pursued at the expense of deepening. This conclusion is perhaps strengthened when one considers the very real difficulties which have been encountered since the Treaty of Maastricht in developing the European Union, and in particular the growing evidence that the financial disciplines which Member Sstates are required to impose on themselves in order to meet the convergence criteria for membership in the first stage of the Single Currency in 1999 are creating social pressures which may be intolerable and which may therefore cause at the very least a delay in the introduction of the Single Currency. These developments in turn cast a shadow over the whole process of European integration, and reinforce the notion that broadening may be more easily achieved than deepening.

If this view proves to be correct, then it must also be likely that further attempts at the integration of national markets will be delayed, partly because of lack of political will to pursue them, partly because of the need to allow time for new Member States to bring their level of development and integration up to that achieved by existing Member States.

2.   THE FUTURE OF FINANCIAL SERVICES

In considering the issues specifically relevant to the development of the Single Market in insurance it is necessary to take account of changes in the structure of the market which have happened since the Single Market Programme began in 1985. Although these changes have taken place in the context of the Single Market Programme, by no means all of them can be considered as being responses to it, and some of those changes have undermined the assumptions on which the original Programme was based.

The Commission's Internal Market Programme started out on the basis of the assumptions (albeit largely unspoken) that financial services, taken as a sector of the market, would continue to operate in much the same way as it had operated for many years past. A simple (perhaps simplistic) description of that mode of operation would be to say that traditionally the different types of financial service, which may for present purposes be characterised as insurance, banking (including deposit services), investment services have tended to operate in more or less sealed compartments. In other words significant numbers of people have wanted only one of these services; the services have not been generally seen as substitutes one for another in the economic sense; there have been relatively few composite groups of companies providing all these services, far less any groups consciously integrating their marketing efforts in relation to different classes of service.

The validity of this simple sketch as a model for the Commission's work may be shown by the elementary fact that the different sectors already identified have been made the subject of separate series of Directives,[1] with no effort to consider the overlap between them, although it is true that the Single Passport home State Regulation system has been consistently adopted in all these areas. This common approach merely reflects the Commission's realisation that similar issues arise in all these sectors. In defence of the fragmented approach it might well be said that the task of taking each sector separately has been quite difficult enough, without trying to deal with the added complexities of integrating the sectors, especially in a marketplace which is rapidly changing and whose future is difficult to predict.

In truth, however, this is a picture which, at least in the United Kingdom, has been increasingly out of date for some years past. A number of important trends may be identified. First, insurance companies have tended to grow larger, partly through organic growth and partly through acquisitions, the July 1996 merger of Royal Insurance and Sun Alliance to form Royal and Sun Alliance plc being only the most topical and conspicuous example. Larger companies of this kind naturally seek to expand their range of activities, but at the same time contribute to an overdue rationalisation of the insurance sector, which has long suffered from serious overcapacity. Second, there is a growing tendency for providers of one kind of financial service to

---

[1] In the case of banking the First Directive, 77/780 of 12 December 1977 OJ L322 17.12.77, the Second Directive, 89/646 of 15 December 1989 OJ L386 30.12.89.

diversify into providing others. Simple examples include the trend towards banks having their own captive insurance companies (and sometimes unit trust companies) and in some cases[2] trying, not necessarily successfully, to provide independent financial advice. Another example is the trend since the Building Societies Act 1986 for these societies, which were originally no more than savings and loan institutions, to provide current account banking facilities and in some cases also to act as insurance brokers or agents. In the late 1980's a major building society, the Abbey National, changed its status to that of a bank. At the time of writing the largest of the building societies, the Halifax, is in the process of doing the same thing, as is another major Building Society, the Alliance and Leicester. Other proposed conversions at the present time include smaller Building Societies such as the Bristol & West and the Northern Rock. In the 1990s the trend has extended to mergers between banks and building societies.[3] This trend, known in France as bancassurance and in Germany as Allfinanz, raises serious questions about the continued appropriateness of treating the different aspects of financial services separately from each other.[4] On the one hand it may be said that under the existing regulatory system businesses which want to offer insurance and banking services are required to do so through separate companies in order to ringfence the regulatory and financial issues arising from the different types of service. On the other hand it is clear that these distinctions are artificial. They result from the regulatory system itself, since it is only that system which creates the requirement for the distinctions. Moreover, companies within the same group (ie with the same parent company) may offer different services, so that the present regime provides only the most formalistic separation of the activities. Moreover, it is unlikely that the majority of consumers understand even the existence of this distinction, far less its importance. It is suggested that the proper way forward in this area is to decide whether at the level of principle the practice of bancassurance ought to be permitted. If the conclusion is that it should be permitted, then it will be necessary to devise a rational regulatory scheme taking account of the issues raised by bancassurance. These would include the need for transparency so that consumers understand that they are not receiving impartial advice when for example they are referred from the

---

2   National Westminster being the most obvious example in the case of banks, whilst the Bradford and Bingley Building Society is the only top ten Building Society to embrace the same principle.

3   The 1995 Lloyd's Bank and Cheltenham and Gloucester Building Society merger is the most high-profile example, though since then the Abbey National has taken over another Building Society, the National and Provincial.

4   Slade, (1993), 3 Ins L + P 45.

banking division of a conglomerate to the insurance division, the need for continued ringfencing of financial resources so that policyholders are not prejudiced by the failure of the banking division and the need to ensure financial stability, the employment of fit and proper persons in responsible positions and the enforcement of appropriate conduct of business rules. None of these tasks is especially difficult, but none of them can be achieved unless the Commission makes a policy decision to treat the financial services sector in this integrated way.

Another interesting feature of the development of bancassurance is that so far there has apparently been no move by insurance companies to take over or create for themselves providers of other kinds of financial services – where conglomerates of this kind have been created this has always been at the instigation of banks which wished to diversify.

This apparent self–denial on the part of insurers is somewhat surprising, since it is not to be supposed that it comes from any altruistic motives. It would be possible to speculate that setting up an insurance–oriented subsidiary is less difficult in regulatory terms, less expensive in terms of capital investment and more likely to produce a reasonable return within a manageable timescale than the setting up by an insurance company of a subsidiary bank. The latter would certainly be very capital intensive. What cannot be doubted is that the financial services market, especially in the United Kingdom, but also to some extent in other countries,[5] is undergoing radical change brought on by market pressures and technological progress. It is far from clear that the existing regulatory framework, either at national level or at European level, is adequate to cope with the kinds of business which will emerge from the current upheaval. It is clearly not acceptable that the development of the market to meet the needs of the 21st Century should be delayed by regulatory systems which were intended, among other things, to facilitate the rational development of the market. It appears that the Commission will face a considerable challenge in developing the structure in time to respond to the commercial changes.

A. The Role of the Commission

The question of the need for changes in the system naturally leads the discussion to a consideration of the role of the Commission. It is of course fundamental that the Commission, as guardian of the Treaties and representative of the central EU interest, has an essential role to play in the development of all aspects of the Internal Market. However, some important

---

5   Slade, above note 4.

political and constitutional questions also arise. These are by no means limited to the development of the insurance sector or even of financial services generally; however, some particular events in these sectors serve to dramatise the issues particularly well.

The first question is as to the extent to which the Commission might be thought to be running ahead of the view of the Member States in pursuing the Internal Market. At the time of writing it is probably fair to say that enthusiasm for the ever closer union among the peoples of Europe envisaged by the recitals to the Treaty of Rome is less strong than it has been for some considerable time. This is perhaps particularly a United Kingdom phenomenon, but there is evidence that in other Member States the popular mood has turned somewhat against such projects as the Single Currency. It may be doubted whether there is at the present time much support for further integration in this area. On the other hand, it might be said that the Internal Market in insurance is more or less complete, so that no further legislation is necessary, assuming that any project for the harmonisation of insurance contract law has been abandoned for the time being. This view is, however, rather contradicted by the observations in the previous section about the need to develop the regulatory structure to take account of the development of bancassurance. It seems that we have here an example of the tendency of regulatory systems to deal with the problems of the past (since they tend to be essentially reactive in nature) rather than anticipating the problems of the future. In a marketplace which is fast-moving and increasingly globalised this threatens to be a serious problem, and it is scarcely necessary to state the advantages which would result if the Commission could make the leap to being pro-active rather than reactive. Unfortunately it is also scarcely necessary to state the most serious obstacle to the making of this change. That obstacle has in fact already been alluded to earlier in this section, when mention was made of the fact that the Commission's awareness of the broader issues is often already several steps ahead of that of the Member States. The notion that the Commission should become even more forward-looking than it already is, whilst admirable in theory, is unlikely to produce good results at the political level.

The second question in this area concerns the way in which the Commission has interpreted the Directives in case of doubt. It is clear that the Commission does have a role to play here: where there is uncertainty about the meaning of a Directive, the natural starting point is to ask the Commission for its view on interpretation. This in turn places a considerable responsibility on the Commission, for in many cases its interpretation is likely to prevail, it being too expensive and too protracted a process to challenge that interpretation. The Commission must therefore be careful to produce interpretations which are simultaneously defensible by reference to the words used in the relevant legislation and sensible by reference to the task of developing the Internal Market. Of course, these two objectives may in some cases appear to be in conflict with each other, in which event the Commission will need to be particularly careful and particularly skilful to avoid giving offence and losing credibility.

B. The Role of the ECJ

As was mentioned in Chapter 1, the ECJ has not to date been called upon to play a major role in the development of the Internal Market in insurance, though of course the co–insurance cases[6] were of considerable significance in the broader context of freedom to provide services. If the Court is to be called upon to take a more active role in the future development of this area, it seems that this is likely to be in the context of allegations that national markets are not being opened up to insurers from other Member States in the way contemplated by the Directives. Given that everybody except Greece has now implemented the Directives, the only real scope left for national authorities to attempt to partition the market is by objecting to insurers from other States which seek to exercise the right of establishment and/or by taking a broad view of the 'general good' exception as a way of denying the freedoms supposedly guaranteed by the Directives.

C. The Role of the Insurance Undertakings

It is worth observing at this point that the development of the Single Market in insurance is also dependent to some extent on the behaviour of the insurance undertakings. If they choose to stick to their own national markets, then no true Single Market can be created. It must also be recognised that they are unlikely to be keen on accepting the risks involved in entering new markets unless there is reasonable prospect of reward. This statement is of course true in all sectors of the economy, and there is little that the Commission can do to help towards satisfying this general condition. To this extent the development of the market is in the hands of wider economic factors.

---

6   Cases 205/84 and 206/84; Lasok 51 MLR 706.

3. PRIORITIES FOR FUTURE ACTION

Looking at the position as it currently stands, it is suggested that there are three possible areas which might be thought to be in need of relatively urgent attention. All have been considered at some length in earlier chapters. They are the 'general good', Intermediaries and Complaints Handling.

A. The General Good

This was considered at length in Chapter 4. It is arguable that the present ambiguity over the scope of this exception is most undesirable because of the opportunities which it creates for Member States to undermine the Single Market principle. On the other hand, it is hard to see how legislation could satisfactorily be drafted to define exhaustively the cases in which derogation from the Single Market principle is to be permitted. On that assumption, the development of the concept in the context of insurance will have to be left to the Court, and it is to be hoped that in practice a very restrictive interpretation will be adopted.

B. Intermediaries

The role and regulation of intermediaries were considered in Chapter 5. This is certainly an area where regulation so far has been very light, perhaps because of the difficulties of harmonising the very different practices found in different Member States. Indeed, the existing Directive[7] concentrates on raising general standards of competence rather than on harmonising practices or domestic regulatory regimes. Given the importance of intermediaries of all kinds in the selling of insurance, and given the difficulties which appear to surround their activities, especially in the United Kingdom, the regulation of intermediaries does appear to be the area of insurance law and practice most ripe for attention.

C. Complaints Handling

This topic was also discussed in Chapter 5. So long as policyholders bought policies almost exclusively within their own jurisdiction, there seemed to be no real need to harmonise the disparate complaints handling systems, but any

---

7   Directive 77/92 of 13 December 1976 OJ L 26 31.01.77.

significant growth in cross–border consumer insurance business inevitably changes this. The position does not appear to have reached crisis point as yet, but it is safe to predict that pressure for reform in this area will increase in the next few years. If the complaints handling schemes are seen as a form of low–level arbitration, then such reform will amount to the creation of a private international law of complaints handling, in which the recognised issues of jurisdiction, choice of law and enforcement of judgments will have to be worked out between the various schemes.

D.   Conclusions

The writing of this book has occupied much of the time since the Third Directives came into force, and at different times during that period very different attitudes to the development of the Single Market have seemed appropriate, ranging from fresh–eyed enthusiasm and optimism to a rather cynical acceptance that no Single Market can possibly be achieved in the foreseeable future. Inevitably, the truth probably lies somewhere in between these two extremes. Much has already been achieved – the regulatory systems have been harmonised, free provision of services is in place and there is now a single passport system. On the other hand, there is a natural limit to what legislation can achieve – it can create a climate in which vigorous enterprise can flourish, but it cannot by itself create that enterprise. Further integrationist legislation is in any event unlikely, both because of the political trends already identified and because other less developed areas must now seem more likely candidates for the attention of the Commission. Although there is a possible argument for the need for further legislation, especially in relation to the three areas identified in the previous paragraph, it seems more likely that this area should and will now be left for some years to develop under the influence of market forces.

Index

For Product Safety Concerns and Information please contact our EU representative GPSR@taylorandfrancis.com Taylor & Francis Verlag GmbH, Kaufingerstraße 24, 80331 München, Germany

Printed and bound by CPI Group (UK) Ltd, Croydon, CR0 4YY
08/05/2025
01864414-0002